D1605119

A FANS' GUIDE

HAWAII FIVE-O

by Cheryl Hollar

Tomahawk Press

First published in 2017 by
Tomahawk Press
PO Box 1236
Sheffield S11 7XU
England

www.tomahawkpress.com

ISBN 13: 978-0-9566834-8-9

Edited by Bruce Sachs
Designed by Tree Frog Communication www.treefrogcommunication.co.uk

Printed in the EU by Gutenberg Press Limited

FOREWORD

I celebrate *Hawaii 5-0*. I celebrate it primarily because of its marvelous producer Peter Lenkov, who got a bug up his nether regions and decided to take one of the episodes I did 37 years ago and tie it into a new episode of the present and by Holy Petunia he did it. I was a scumbag evil doer in the past but fortunately was kept alive by the grace of the authorities not recognizing my innate evil, which would only be bared by the brilliance of the present day cast, Peter Lenkov and modern forensics. That's what I find fascinating in the transition to modern times

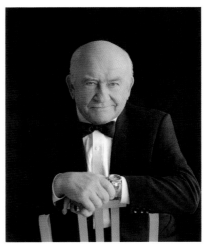

– you never realize who will be a genius at any given moment. Thirty-seven years ago, Jack Lord was the resident genius and everyone else took turns at saying, "duh!" Not so now. They're all capable of stealing your wrist watch when you're looking elsewhere. As a performer who has bestrode both worlds, I was quite taken by the sharpness and acuity of all the performers including the supporting cast. As I said, any one of them could rip off your watch. Being a senior citizen, I had to be sure I had my specs on when they were near me. They're all sharp and far too clever. I have to run to catch up. They're an exhilarating bunch and a joy to be around. My special thanks to Peter Lenkov and Scott Caan.

Cheryl Hollar's book presents this in sparkling fashion. It's a loving tribute to the series and will be a great read for the fans!

Edward Asner

INTRODUCTION

It's been my privilege to play roles in both the original *Hawaii Five-O* as Ben Kokua and the 2010 reboot as Mamo Kahike. Obviously, if it had not been for the huge success of Leonard Freeman's original concept, there would be no reboot with the appeal to reach a whole new generation of young viewers.

My hope is that this success will carry on for years to come. The enthusiasm of the series' network of fans continues to be astounding in its effect on Hawaii's social and economic development. We are blessed to have so many dedicated fans of the series, and this book from Cheryl Hollar is a book for the fans – a book to enhance their enjoyment of the series.

I am pleased that my friend took the time to research and write such a book, and I highly recommend this book to all who enjoy the series.

Al Harrington, 2016

A NOTE FROM THE AUTHOR

This book has been a six-year labor of love. It is just a glimpse, nothing more, nothing less, into the behind-the-scenes world of a television series and its reboot. And it's an unofficial "tour book," if you will, to the beautiful islands that are Hawaii. It's simply written – unofficially – for the fans, and if there is any copyright infringement of any kind, it is unintentional. It is meant to simply be a fun look for fans into the world that is *Hawaii Five-0*. In researching and writing this book, I had the honor to meet and get to know so many wonderful people, and  I thank all of them for their time and donations of pictures, stories, etc. It is all most appreciated.

This book is dedicated lovingly to my twin sister, Meryl Hollar, who is a constant encourager to my writing career. "Thank you. I love you."

Cheryl Hollar, 2017
cherylfhollar@yahoo.com

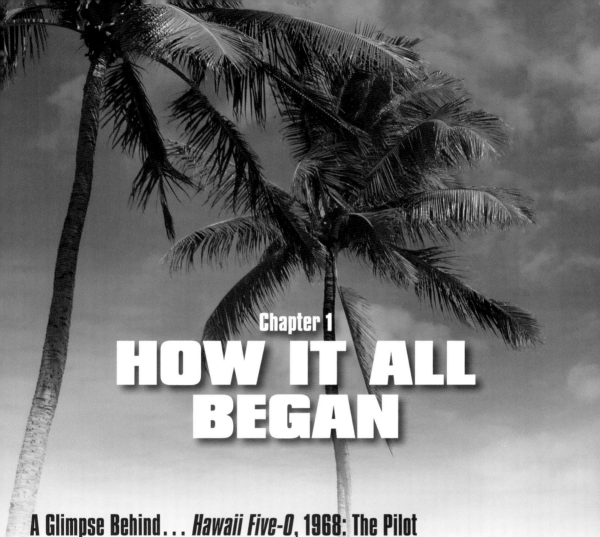

Chapter 1
HOW IT ALL BEGAN

A Glimpse Behind... *Hawaii Five-O*, 1968: The Pilot

While recuperating from a heart attack at his mother-in-law's Hawaiian home in 1967, Executive Producer Leonard Freeman began working on the development of a new television series he planned to call *The Man.*[1] The concept arguably came from a meeting Freeman had with his actor friend, Richard Boone. As the concept of the series progressed, Freeman approached Iranian-American Director Reza Badiyi about shooting footage for the opening sequence of his potential series. Freeman gave Badiyi just five days to shoot as much sequence footage as he could. The only request was that the footage be symbolic of Hawaii, where the series would be filmed. For Badiyi, the best symbol of Hawaii was the surf, so he went on a quest for the "best waves" on Oahu. As a result, Badiyi was responsible for one of the most famous title sequences in television history the moment that "big wave" hit the CBS airwaves on September 20, 1968 at 8 pm. No one, not even Badiyi himself, could pinpoint the exact location of the big wave sequence that identified the series, but Badiyi and "Surfing" magazine Senior Editor Sam George narrowed the probable location as Rock Pile at Ehukai Beach Park on Oahu's North Shore. No matter the wave location, there was speculation that Freeman agreed to pay Badiyi $200 every time that wave splashed onto the small screen, an agreement that worked well until the series faltered during the first season when it failed to crack the Top 30. Freeman,

Jack Lord (center) in a 1964 photo from a rodeo tour he took following the demise of the 1962-63 ABC-TV *Stoney Brook* series (anonymous fan contribution)

certain his series would be cancelled, then offered Badiyi a flat $5,000 for use of the wave sequence. However, twelve seasons and waves of repeats later, Badiyi surely cringed every time the sequence was broadcast. It is more likely, however, that Badiyi's "so-what" attitude toward life's disappointments kept him from being too upset at what might have been. Most probably, he never looked back.[2]

Sometime prior to pitching his new series idea to CBS, Freeman got the stamp of approval from the Governor and the Mayor of Hawaii and decided to call the series *Hawaii Five-O,* simply in honor of the 50th state. CBS executives were not an easy sell however, and one of them reportedly said, "People who have been to Hawaii have already seen the place. And those who have never been there obviously don't care. So why should anyone watch this thing?" Nonetheless, CBS asked Freeman if he would script six episodes for them.[3] At last, Freeman had his shot, and that was all he needed for the airing of at least the first few episodes of his new series.

The final production decision made was the choice of a theme song. For that task, Freeman turned to Morton Stevens, who was CBS' Director of Music, West Coast Operations. Stevens' wife, Anne, urged him to write an original piece for the new series, a theme for which she would have final approval, even before the piece was pitched to Freeman. Stevens agreed but effort after effort was rejected by Anne until he could stand it no more. At his wit's end and during a heated argument with his wife, he angrily pounded out what was to become the classic Emmy-nominated iconic theme of *Hawaii Five-O.*[4]

Chapter 1 – HOW IT ALL BEGAN

Waves of the North Shore (from the author's personal collection)

Freeman found his leading man in actor Jack Lord, whom he had worked with previously in the unsold TV pilot *Grand Hotel*.[5] Lord was to play Detective Steve McGarrett, head of the Five-O State Police Force. Under his command were Detectives Danny Williams (James MacArthur, played by Tim O'Kelly in the pilot), Chin Ho Kelly (Kam Fong), and Kono Kalakaua (Zulu). Something Freeman insisted on from the start of the series was that his characters remain somewhat anonymous to viewers. They were never to have a "past." *Hawaii Five-O* writer Jerome Coopersmith revealed in "Mystery Scene's" 2004 Spring issue that Freeman "often told me, 'I don't want to know anything about McGarrett's personal life. He only exists as a cop.'" James MacArthur confirmed this in the "Honolulu Star-Bulletin" in 1996: "You never saw us at home or doing something outside of police business. We weren't a show with a lot of laughs either. When you do a long-term series you have to look for truth in your character. You want people to know what they're going to get the next week and have them looking forward to what they're going to get. Consistency and continuity are crucial."

Locals loved Freeman's series tribute to the Island. When Jack Lord filmed that now-famous title sequence balcony scene at the Penthouse level, Diamond Head corner of the Ilikai Hotel[6] sometime prior to the airing of Freeman's new series, then Ilikai PR exec Bobbie Kane said, "Honolulu couldn't have been more proud. Locals excitedly gathered around as Hollywood came to the Ilikai for the second time."[7]

The series Freeman thought would not last past Season One ended up with the distinction of being one of the longest first-run police procedurals in television history (surpassed only by *Law and Order).* It cracked the Top 20 in its second season, moved to the Top 10 in its third, and by the fifth season was listed as one of the top three most-watched shows on television. The series finale, "Woe to Wo Fat," aired in April, 1980.[8]

OW • DID YOU KNOW • DID YOU KNOW • DID YOU KNOW • DID YOU KNOW • DID YOU

The name Chin Ho came from Chinn Ho, the owner of the Ilikai Hotel.[9]

McGarrett was a Naval Intelligence Officer before he became head of Five-O. In fact, he was in the reserves and went on active duty from time to time to assist the Navy or Coast Guard on special cases.[10]

The name Wo Fat came from the former Wo Fat Restaurant in Chinatown, Honolulu.[11]

The phrase "Book 'em Danno" was not only said to Danny. McGarrett used the 'Book 'em' phrase to others on the team as well.[12]

Writer Jerome Coopersmith, who wrote for the series from his home in Long Island, New York for six years, based his visuals of the Island from his visits to Puerto Rico.[13]

Morton Stevens took the notes of the Hawaii Five-O *theme song as his license plate number: AACEDA.*[14]

A wonderful, in-depth, behind-the-scenes look at the original Five-O *and its actors can be found in* Booking Hawaii Five-O *by Karen Rhodes.*

Left: Alex O'Loughlin and Norman Reedus (Anton Hesse) shoot a scene from the reboot pilot (photo credit: David B. Johnson, Saber Ops). Right: Kualoa Ranch, Ko'olau Mountain Range where reboot pilot was shot (photo credit: David B. Johnson, Saber Ops)

A Glimpse Behind... *Hawaii Five-O* Reboot, 2010: The Pilot

The pilot for the series reboot aired exactly 42 years from the premiere date of the original series (CBS, September 20, 2010, 10 pm.). Word first came about 2008 via "The Hollywood Reporter" that CBS was developing a new take on *Hawaii Five-O* with *Criminal Minds* Showrunner Ed Bernero, with the storyline centering on lead character Chris McGarrett, son of Detective Steve McGarrett (from the original series).[15] No further word came from the project until late 2009, when "The Hollywood Reporter" confirmed that CBS had indeed given a pilot commitment for the series reboot. However, there were changes to the original announcement. *CSI: NY* Executive Producer Peter Lenkov, along with *Star Trek/Transformers* writers Alex Kurtzman and Roberto Orci, were to serve as Executive Producers of the potential series, and the story would center around the original character Steve McGarrett.[16] Word was that Showrunner Lenkov also wanted his new series to honor the original. In November, 2010, he told the "Star-Advertiser's" Vicki Viotti, "I was a huge fan of the original show, so I feel like there are a lot of elements I took or cherry-picked from the original show that I thought was no reason to fix or change. I wanted to sort of carry on and keep that legacy alive. I wanted to keep the spirit of the show alive. That's key to me, just the idea of who these characters are and what they stand for and why they do what they do. If you keep that spirit alive, I think you're honoring the original show."[17] Mike Gordon of the "Advertiser" reported a month later that Lenkov had watched the original

McGarrett (Alex O'Loughlin) on the right side of balcony of the Ilikai Hotel (photo credit: Stephanie G. Spangler)

series with his father, "who considered *'Five-O'* his favorite show." Lenkov had also shared his father's story with Kurtzman and Orci when he pitched it to the pair ("Star-Advertiser," December 29, 2010). Kurtzman was touched by the pitch and told the "Advertiser," "We knew instantly that he was coming from an honorable and emotional place."[18]

The trio of Executive Producers decided to keep portions of the title sequence, including that big wave, as well as the theme song. Leonard Freeman continued to be honored as creator of the series. They also decided to re-create that balcony scene, at the urging of Hawaii-based Location Manager Stephanie G. Spangler, whose father was the very first, though unofficial, Location Manager for the original *Hawaii Five-O*. Consequently, the actor hired to play Steve McGarrett (Alex O'Loughlin) was filmed on exactly the same balcony as Jack Lord. Terry Dowsett, General Manager of the Ilikai, recollected the shooting of that scene:

"We were contacted by the Producers of the upcoming re-creation of *Hawaii Five-O*. They wanted to do various photography of the new stars for PR purposes, and they wanted to replicate the opening shot that zooms in on McGarrett on the lanai. The PR shots took nearly a full day, and the next day was dedicated to the balcony shot. It began very early in the morning. With current flight regulations, the film company had to get approval to have a helicopter fly over land and close to our building. Police had to block off all vehicle and pedestrian access in the rear of the building for several hours. All people in the surrounding buildings were also notified of the disruption and reason for helicopter activity. After the helicopter shot with Alex, things resorted to normal on the ground, but the photo shoot with the rest of the key cast members continued on the same lanai. I was amazed at the significant amount of manpower, coordination, and cost involved for what ended up as seconds on film."[19]

The reboot series did have some deviations from the original. For instance, the title in the original series was a simple representation of the 50th state whereas, in the reboot, the title came from McGarrett's high school football jersey number "5-0,"[20] signifying a nickname of sorts that McGarrett's father had given his family – "the 5-0's" (transplanted locals, if you will, to the 50th state). Another deviation involved character changes between the original series and the reboot. The character of "Kono Kalakaua," though retaining the same name in the reboot, became a female role (with Grace Park playing the part). The history of the selection of the Governor's Five-O Task Force was never revealed in the original series. But, in the reboot, decorated Navy SEAL Lieutenant Commander Steve McGarrett returned home to Hawaii to bury his murdered father and was persuaded by the Governor to head her Task Force. McGarrett also hand-picked his own team: Officer Danny Williams (Scott Caan) a transplanted cop from New Jersey who couldn't see eye-to-eye with McGarrett from the beginning; former Honolulu Police Department (HPD) Officer Chin Ho Kelly (Daniel Dae Kim), a cop McGarrett had known since high school who had fallen from grace with HPD through no fault of his own; and Police Academy Cadet Kono Kalakaua, Chin Ho's cousin. Another deviation from the original series was the development of the characters themselves. Where Freeman purposefully decided not to give his characters a past, Lenkov most decidedly did. Lenkov told the "Advertiser" in November, 2010, "What I think we're most proud of is our character work. And I think comedy, which is rare in the procedural dramas, is a big deal for us."

The last letter of the Hawaii Five-0 reboot is a zero instead of a capital letter (as in the original Five-O).

McGarrett used the catchphrase from the original series, "Book 'em Danno" in the pilot of the reboot.

Officer Kalakaua had not yet graduated from the Police Academy in the pilot, though she did unofficially graduate in Episode 2.[21]

Saber Ops (http://www.militarytechadvisor.com) was the military advisor team for Season One of the reboot.[22]

Chapter 2
ON LOCATION

A Glimpse At... Location, Location, Location

H awaii not only provides *Hawaii Five-0* with a canvas of exquisite beauty, but the State itself is just as much a "star" of the series as any of its lead actors. The Hawaiian Islands, in fact, have been no strangers to Hollywood. In 2013, the Hawaii Film Office announced its celebration of 100 years in the film industry, with *Hawaii Five-0* being one of the most notable television Productions ever shot in the State.[1] Filming in Hawaii has been like nowhere else in the world. In September, 1999, Tim Ryan wrote a piece for the "Star-Bulletin" (now "Star-Advertiser") entitled "'Five-O' Put Spotlight on Hawaii." In the article, then Hawaii Film Office Manager Georgette Deemer was quoted as saying, "Hands down, 'Hawaii Five-0' created Hawaii's television industry." Rose Freeman, Creator/Producer Leonard Freeman's wife, also said, "The show brought Hawaii to the world and the world then visited Hawaii."[2]

When *Hawaii Five-O* launched in 1967, there were no studios or sound stages in the State. In fact, when the production initially arrived on the Islands, Earle Spangler, a retired Naval Captain and realtor, helped the Producers find locations around Oahu for series episodes. In the beginning of the series, it was the job of the Art Director and Production Manager to find shooting locations on the Island but, as Spangler got to know many of the members of the production team socially, they'd ask him from time to time for shooting location ideas. In fact, Spangler found their very first sound stage - an Army warehouse at Pearl Harbor. Back then, there wasn't much at Pearl Harbor, and there definitely weren't any freeways. Though he was never given the title of "Location Manager," that's just what Spangler was. He was the very first Location Manager in Hawaii. It was (and is) the Location Manager's job to find sites for each episode of a series according to the show's scripts. As requests for houses on the beach came in, Spangler used his social contacts to get the producers into Kama'aina homes on Kahala Avenue. Back then, location fees consisted of a warm "mahalo" (thank you) with a gift basket of whiskey or wine and a bouquet of roses.[3]

It was only fitting that, when Spangler's son, Randy, returned from Vietnam, he became *Hawaii Five-O's* first "known" official Location Manager. The series was Randy's first client, and he was Location Manager for its remaining 10 years on the air.[4] Today, Randy is known as being highly trusted, having the key to every gate on the Island, and his word is gold. Scouting is Randy's passion. Being an outdoorsman, a self-professed "explorer," and a lover of off-road vehicles, dune buggies, dirt bikes, and boats, with a love for meeting and working with all kinds of people, it was only fitting that he'd fall into location management. For the series *Lost,* he even managed to transform Diamond Head Crater into an Iraqi prison camp.[5]

Randy's sister, Stephanie G. Spangler, President of the Hawaii Film Authority, started working in the family business in 1977 when she was thrown onto a Movie of the Week with no experience. She managed to handle the job quite well and started building a reputation in Hawaii. In fact, she and Randy have been the "go-to" people for *Hawaii Five-O* locations since the early days of the series. When the notoriety of *Five-O* began a trend in television production for the Islands, it was Stephanie who found locations for the many commercials being shot in Hawaii. She opened up the outer Islands to commercial production by working with the airlines and hotels to make deals and by creating packages of productions to take to the outer limits of the Island chain. For years, she was a Production Supervisor/Location Manager on commercial spots, working with top production houses and advertising agencies. She oftentimes had to work single handed, and her jobs varied from that of Production Supervisor/ Location Manager to 2nd AD (Assistant Director) to work in styling and craft services. These days, Stephanie is so connected to location management that when she watches television, she's constantly recognizing background shots in a series. Both Stephanie and Randy have used locations which are considered great and unusual "finds" that they refuse to share with anyone, one such "find" being a "trailer park" for the pilot of the *Five-0* reboot. Hawaii has no trailer parks, so to scout out a location that might double as one was huge. To secure it, Stephanie had to pay residents a nuisance fee, plus one month's rental on the apartment unit she used in the scene, plus a location fee to the owner of the entire property.[6]

Both Randy and Stephanie agree that being in the location management business is not always easy. In the early, early days of *Five-O*, back when Earle was Location Manager, the Pearl Harbor warehouse he located for the series' Production Office had some problems. It leaked. And when it rained, plastic cartons stood everywhere. Once, there was a landslide in the area, and the crew was stranded in the valley. In addition, there were many, many Mongoose, so many that the crew gave them names. There were also numerous centipedes. And there were few location choices available in those days. Randy surmised that an entire season's worth of episodes were probably filmed at the Ilikai Hotel. Sites that were used for the Production back in the 1960's and 1970's included Waimea Valley on the North Shore, which has been described as a spiritual place on the Island. Many episodes of the series revolved around the military, and those were usually located around Pearl Harbor. Series location personnel would work with the US Department of Defense at those times. *Five-O* shot often in a 1930's wooden two-story apartment house sandwiched between two newer buildings in Chinatown. Often, locals would accept no pay from the production when their properties were used on the series. The show itself represented the marketability of the State of Hawaii, and everyone wanted to donate the use of lands and houses for the sake of "showing off" the State. Jack Lord himself was named Marketer of the Year for two years in a row for the impact of *Hawaii Five-O* on the marketing of Hawaii.[7]

Some of the writers for the original series were located in Los Angeles, and some were in New York. In order to get ideas for episodes, these writers were sent clippings from magazines and newspapers with the latest news from Hawaii. Sometimes, their work had to be translated into "Hawaiian." For instance, if a scene called for a fancy yacht, the Hawaiian translation might be a fishing boat, because of the cost ratio. There was no Marina Del Ray, no Newport, not even big Bel Air homes on the water. Such homes would be way too costly for translation into "Hawaiian."[8]

The *Five-0* Reboot

Though things have changed over the years, the Spangler name is still synonymous with *Five-0*. When CBS gave the go-ahead for the reboot in February, 2010, Stephanie was asked by a Producer from CBS to enlist as Location Manager. After breaking down the script and identifying the number of locations needed, she attached her ideas of possible sites from hundreds of references in her files. Due to the significant land development over the years, things had obviously changed in Hawaii. Stephanie had no choice but to re-scout locations for their "present-day" look. She also worked very closely with the Production Designer for visualization ideas to present to the Director who, for the pilot, was Len Wiseman.

> I was really thrilled with the *Hawaii Five-0* pilot. I thought it was just a great show with a great Production team, cast, and crew. The memory of that technical maneuver with the balcony shot was the most memorable thing I'll take away from it. That shot wasn't at all easy.
> *Stephanie G. Spangler,* Hawaii Five-0 *Reboot Pilot Location Manager*

One of the interesting problems she encountered was the location of McGarrett's house. It became evident during the house-hunting process that Wiseman wanted a house on the beach, but every photo Stephanie presented to him was shot down. She couldn't figure this out until she had the opportunity to speak and scout with the Director one-on-one and started going over images in her mind, along with actual data images, to try and put together what Wiseman was really looking for. One day as they were scouting the Manoa neighborhood, with the fabulous cottage-style homes, Stephanie suggested that a "Manoa style" cottage on the beach might be what he was seeking. He agreed, and she showed him an archived file of the Bayer Estate in Aina

Haina. He loved it, and the site of McGarrett's house was chosen.

Danno's architectural, Polynesian detailed apartment seen in the first three seasons of the series was found behind the Ilikai, just five minutes from the *Five-0* Production Office at the Hilton Hawaiian Village, in a corner unit on the ground floor. The only problem was that the apartment was so small that the Director could not get a camera crew inside. Wiseman rose to the

Film crew for pilot of reboot outside the Ai'olani Building, Hawaii Five-0 Headquarters (photo credit: Stephanie G. Spangler)

challenge and found a corner window facing out. He shot through the window, then through the doorway. His unique approach worked well.

Locating the perfect spot for Five-0 Headquarters was also a challenge. Original production ideas Stephanie had received from the producers called for a modern, glass, high-tech office building on the ocean. This didn't translate well into "Hawaiian." However, Stephanie was familiar with the history of territorial architecture seen in the original series and suggested the use of the

Above: Reboot crew prepares for a chase scene in the reboot pilot (photo credit: Stephanie G. Spangler).

Above: Len Wiseman (second from right) and team scout for perfect reboot pilot locations (photo credit: Stephanie G. Spangler). Below: Helicopter comes in for its first pass at balcony shot with McGarrett at Ilikai Hotel (photo credit: Stephanie G. Spangler)

Chapter 2 – ON LOCATION

Helicopter arrives at Ilikai Hotel for balcony shot of McGarrett (photo credit: Stephanie G. Spangler)
Inset: Helicopter moves in on McGarrett on balcony of the Ilikai Hotel
(photo credit: Stephanie G. Spangler)

main Post Office in Downtown Honolulu as the site for the Five-0 offices. She had previously used a 5,000 square foot area in the building for indoor catering in 1996, when there were talks about a possible reboot starring Gary Busey.[9] By 2010, she could no longer find access to the space, nor could she find anyone else that knew anything about it. However, one Sunday afternoon, she took it upon herself to walk about the Post Office building and look for the area in question. She couldn't see into the windows but was able to hold her camera high over her head and use a wide angle lens to shoot a picture. After doing this to several of the building's windows, she finally found the space she had remembered. It was being used as storage for boxes from the Post Office. The floor was black lacquer, and the high architectural-designed windows were still in place. Locating the room, though, was just the beginning. Stephanie next

Reboot crew sets up for shot on USS Missouri, Ford Island (photo credit: Stephanie G. Spangler)

had to meet with the Postal System's powers that be to try and gain access and permission to use it. She then had to go back to the producers and the director of the reboot to get them to see that this would be a perfect location for Five-0 Headquarters. Once they saw it for themselves, they were convinced of the location, and Stephanie next had to go through five different agencies to knock down a wall and put up a doorway to facilitate access for all of the production equipment, crew, etc. It took weeks to decorate the space and get it ready for the end result.[10]

The producers fell in love with Stephanie's next suggestion. She asked if they would be interested in re-creating the opening credit balcony scene of Jack Lord at the Ilikai (also known as the *"Hawaii Five-O* Hotel").[11] They jumped at the chance to reshoot this iconic scene, using the exact balcony where Jack Lord stood back in 1968. Getting the final shot, however, was a big deal that involved layers and layers of preparation. It was shot on the last day of filming for the pilot episode, and permission to use that particular balcony was not secured until 7 pm the night before. Since the owner of the particular balcony for filming was a Japanese national, Stephanie had to go through the realtor of the apartment where the balcony was located in order to find the owner in Japan and ask his permission to use his balcony. Eighteen Honolulu Police

Above: Reboot crew sets up for a "cargument" (photo credit: Stephanie G. Spangler). Below: Len Wiseman maps out the fight scene between Victor Hesse and McGarrett on the docks (photo credit: Stephanie G. Spangler)

Above: Reboot crew at McGarrett's house (photo credit: Stephanie G. Spangler). Below: Reboot crew sets up a scene inside the McGarrett house (photo credit: Stephanie G. Spangler)

Department officers lined the streets of Ala Moana Boulevard between 5:30 and 6 am on the day of shooting. Traffic had to be stopped from all streets in the area connecting to the street the helicopter was to fly over. Aerial flight patterns were cleared, and barricades through all the harbor streets were placed to stop people from parking in the area. The University of Hawaii football team, The Warriors, came down and manned posts on the ground, along with *Five-0* Production Assistants, to stop the public from walking through an estimated 90 different places on the harbor streets and public right-of-ways off the beach. People had to be redirected to different places. For safety's sake, the helicopter company had to make sure not one single person or vehicle that wasn't with the Production was underneath the flight pattern. In addition, all hotels and apartment buildings in the area had to sign-off for permission to shoot in that spot, and the hotels had to send out notices to every one of their guests to let them know about the filming and to request that the guests stay off the balconies. Stephanie also had to get permission from the Harbor Master. Things were a lot more intense than they had been in 1968. The FAA did not sign off until the morning of the shoot. They had to see all plans and review location and set-up before the FAA would give approval. The FAA signed off on the helicopter shot at 8:15 am, and a chopper immediately took off from Honolulu International Airport to make the first-run shot. The cost of attempting that helicopter shot on the balcony, with or without success, was around $28,000.[12]

> When they shot the pilot, the excitement on the Island was unbelievable. Everybody loves *Five-0*. Look at what the show's done for the economy. I think the remake has put Hawaii back on the map, and that's why hotels are booked solid in Waikiki.
> *Stephanie G. Spangler*

Another memorable reboot location spot for Spangler was the USS Missouri on Ford Island. The most difficult maneuver was just getting the crew on the Island. Everyone wanted to drive on, so Stephanie had to get all drivers' licenses and car license numbers. Then, she actually had to stand at the gate around 4 am with the guards to "okay" everyone as they passed through.[13]

Once the pilot was shot, Stephanie's work was done. Jim Triplett took over where she left off and began finding locations for the Hawaii Five-0 reboot. (He did this through Season Three). For location of some scenes, there was no need to venture outside the studio at all. These "permanent" sets included Five-0 headquarters, autopsy, the police station interior, the Navy communication center, and the interior of McGarrett's house. Though the house was filmed at the Bayer Estate in Season One, due to the complexity of breaking down and setting it up over a period of time, the "house" eventually moved to the studio, where a porch was built with a translight giving the illusion of the beach outside.[14] However, exterior filming resumed at the house in Season Four and both interior and exterior shots resumed at the house in Seasons Five and Six.

In Season Three, Episode 21 "Imi loko ka 'uhane" (Seek Within One's Soul), Triplett had the unenviable task of finding a hotel for a scene where McGarrett would jump off a balcony into a pool. In the script, McGarrett left one hotel room for another one where he jumped over a balcony. Requirements were for Triplett to locate two identical hotel rooms on the same hallway, with at least one having a sliding glass door off the back into the pool. The pool also had to have a safe height and depth for the stuntman to make the jump. In addition, Triplett had to get permission from the owner of whatever hotel he chose, as well as City permits to shoot there. In the end, Triplett settled on an apartment building to double as a hotel in order to accommodate all the necessary requirements.[15]

As the series was renewed for a Fourth, Fifth, and Sixth Season, Timmy Chinn became Location Manager and experienced his own set of challenges. For instance, Season Five's Episode 16, "Nanahu" (Embers) called for a burnt townhouse, which is pretty rare on Oahu, considering that by law, those houses are demolished as quickly as possible. Needless to say, it took a while to find such a house. In addition, Chinn had to find a matching house that wasn't burnt for the before and after scenes. As it turned out, Chinn located both houses nearby each other and within a couple of miles from the studio. One of the more difficult assignments for Chinn was not in finding a particular location, but in making the location work. For instance, coffee plantations on Oahu are under quarantine, meaning that filming on one is out of the question. The problem with filming on one of these plantations is the risk of getting bugs into the fields that could be easily transmitted from one coffee farm to another. To solve his dilemma, Chinn found a group at the University of Hawaii called HARC (Hawaii Agricultural Research Center). This group grows coffee and chocolate for research. The group was kind enough to allow filming at one of their locations. Even then though, there were restrictions. The crew had to wear plain clothes and were not allowed to go from one coffee farm to another. They also could not bring in raw coffee beans. The Director of HARC had a big concern about the possibility of transmitting the aforementioned bug. Chinn also discovered that sometimes locations just need to be built, and he did just that in the Season Five premiere "A'ohe Kahi e Pe'e Ai" (Nowhere to Hide) when he transformed Diamond Head Crater into an isolated, top-secret government facility complete with barbed wire fence in the middle of nowhere. In order to do this, Chinn had to deal with three or four government agencies, including the National Guard and the Department of Defense. Since Diamond Head is a State Monument that attracts thousands of visitors on a daily basis, this shot also required good traffic control and coordination. But Chinn made it work.[16]

W • DID YOU KNOW • DID YOU KNOW • DID YOU KNOW • DID YOU KNOW • DID YOU K

Location scouting for the original Five-O was done with a Lincoln Towncar and a Polaroid Camera.[17]

The McGarrett shot on the Ilikai balcony for the reboot took around 12 helicopter passes within an hour-and-a-half shooting time.[18]

Ka'a'awa Ranch is a well-known film and television "backlot" nowadays. It doubled as North Korea in the pilot of the reboot.[19]

Stephanie G. Spangler was the first Location Manager to discover and use Ka'a'awa Valley as a location site.[20]

An old warehouse with grungy containers was the "at sea" location in the reboot for the huge fight scene between McGarrett and Victor Hesse.[21]

The "team" of an episode's Director, the Producer, Production Designer, Director of Photography, First A. D. , and Location Manager scout around Oahu in a van, taking photos of possible location sites for the Hawaii Five-0 *reboot.[22]*

Wo Fat's luxury Hong Kong apartment in Season Two, Episode 22 ("Ua Hopu" Caught) of the reboot is actually a luxury suite at the Trump Hotel.[23]

In Season Three, Episode 20 ("Olelo Pa'a" The Promise), the Flying R Ranch in the North Shore's Waialua doubles as the LZ (Landing Zone) for a HALO jump McGarrett makes in a flashback to North Korea and as a terrorist camp in North Korea. A hunting lodge at the top of the mountain doubles as a ranch house in Montana.[24]

Ninety percent of the McGarrett/Danno carguments "inside" the Camaro are shot on a stage with movie projectors all around.[25]

In Season Four, Episode 21 "Makani 'olu a holo malie" (Fair Winds and Flowing Seas), the Afghanistan village was built at Diamond Head Crater.[26]

Maunawili, on Oahu's windward side, is a jungle area that has been used as a location many times in the Five-0 reboot, including Season Three, Episode 10 "Huaka'i Kula" (Field Trip), when it was used as Grace's girl scout camp.[27]

The Shriners Beach Club in Waimanalo served as a beach house compound in Season Five, Episode 4 "Ka Noe'au" (The Painter).[28]

Kono's wedding in the Season Five cliffhanger and the Season Six premiere took place at the Royal Hawaiian Golf Club in Maunawili.[29]

One of the most challenging locations for Chinn to locate for Season Five was the swimming pool used to do some of the water work for Episode 23 "Mo'o 'olelo Pu" (Sharing Traditions) where Kono was lost at sea.[30]

Aunt Deb (Carol Burnett) was married (to Frankie Valli) at the Royal Hawaiian Hotel in Season Five, Episode Eight, "Ka Hana Malu" (Inside Job).[31]

Most of the beautiful mansions seen in the series are in Kahala or Portlock.[32]

Chapter 3
ON LOCATION

A Glimpse At... *Hawaii Five-0*, Hawaiian Culture, and Blessings

Before shooting begins on any fabulous Hawaiian locations on any season of *Hawaii Five-0*, a traditional Hawaiian blessing is pronounced by a kahu, or Hawaiian minister. This was true, even for the original *Five-0,* which was blessed by Kahu Abraham Kahikina Akaka[1] of the Kawaiaha'o Church in Honolulu. And, just like the original, the producers of the reboot want to honor Hawaii and its culture as much as possible by pronouncing a Hawaiian blessing at the beginning of each season. This prospect would be quite daunting if it were not for people like Kahu Blaine Kamalani Kia, who has been one of *Hawaii Five-0's* Cultural Advisors over the years. It was Kia's job as Cultural Advisor to keep *Hawaii Five-0* as authentic and as accurate to the Hawaiian tradition as possible. A big chunk of what that involved included the Hawaiian language and the portrayal of the Hawaiian way of life. Thus, each episode of the reboot carries a title in both Hawaiian and English. Similarly, the true Hawaiian way of life is very laid back, consciously making every day a "long day."

Kia, who pronounced the Season Three blessing for *Hawaii Five-0,* sums up the meaning of the Hawaiian blessing, "One of the traditions of Hawaii is that when newcomers or strangers come into our land, it's always good to get a blessing from the people of the land, to welcome you in their traditional way. So, we welcome the newcomer or the stranger that comes from overseas in a ceremony, and in that ceremony is a 'blessing.' This is especially true if they will be interacting with the locals. Sometimes people have different things to offer, and personalities and characters can be conflicting to the way we do things here. So, it's always important to find a way to try to get everybody on the same page. That's what blessings help to do. They help get these cultural people together and try to unite them so that it can be for the betterment of whatever the work or cause is that's being blessed at the moment."[2] According to Kahu Kelekona Bishaw, who pronounced the blessing for Season One, "We [Hawaiians] really believe in what we do. We're asking God for His blessing upon the people, to keep everybody

Daniel Dae Kim (on motorcycle) prepares for first-shot scene of Hawaii Five-0 reboot as Peter Lenkov and Scott Caan look on (photo courtesy of George F. Lee, "Honolulu Star Advertiser")

safe, and all those kinds of things."[3] Kahu Curtis Pa'alua Kwai Fong Kekuna, who pronounced the Season Two blessing for the reboot concurs, "Hawaii believes in blessing, and it is one of the most Christian places in the world. Hawaiians bless all kinds of events – from weddings to ribbon cuttings - all the time and anywhere, from business openings to house groundbreakings to luaus. It's a very common practice."[4] Depicting the culture of Hawaii and keeping its traditions alive is what *Hawaii Five*-0, and all productions in Hawaii for that matter, do. According to Bishaw, "A blessing is not a 'have to do' thing but it's a good thing to do. And there's no 'right' way to do it. Each kahu has his own "signature blessing," if you will. And, each blessing is given in Hawaiian and in English, but usually, mostly in English."

The Season One blessing went like this: Call time was 5:30 am on the morning of July 10, 2010. Bishaw, of the Kamehameha Schools, along with the new cast, crew, producers, etc. were all present on the grounds of the Hilton Hawaiian Village Hotel. It was the first TV series blessing in which Bishaw had ever participated. "It was a big event. Police Chief Louis M. Kealoha from the Hawaii Police Department was there, along with a few of his staff members. The ceremony itself probably took about 10 minutes at the most. Right after

Alex O'Loughlin prepares for first day of shooting Hawaii Five-0 reboot (photo courtesy of George F. Lee, "Honolulu Star Advertiser")

we did the blessing, I asked the cast to untie the maile lei. You don't cut the maile lei with scissors. As for the blessing itself, I just began by giving a quick explanation of why we're doing this and what is involved in it. The cast, especially, would not be familiar with this kind of ceremony. To them, and to anybody else, once I explained what we were doing, they understood, and it had some meaning to them. I then talked about things that connect us to Hawaii. I always like to talk about connection instead of disconnection. I also always use wooden bowls made from woods that are indigenous to Hawaii. That keeps us connected to the land. In Hawaii, the land is very special. Then, there's the water. Water always speaks to life refreshing and new life. And the other part of giving a blessing for me is the Bible. The Scripture that I read (in Hawaiian and in English) was from the Book of Psalms (Psalm 118). It said, 'This is the day the Lord has made; let us rejoice and be glad in it.' (New International Version) I'm part Hawaiian, so I want a connection to Hawaii and also to the Bible. Call it a Christian Hawaiian blessing." Immediately after this very first blessing, as has been the case in every blessing of the series since, *Hawaii Five-0* went straight into production. Bishaw was invited to watch. And what was the very first scene shot? It was McGarrett and Danno driving the Camaro up to the Hilton Hawaiian, Chin in tow on a motorcycle. The three then gave chase to a suspect. To Bishaw's surprise, this scene only lasted 10-15 seconds on the air.[5]

Because Bishaw was unavailable when the time rolled around for giving the Season Two blessing, that honor went to Kekuna, of the Kawaiaha'o Church - the same church where Akaka (who blessed the original *Five-O)* was kahu. Call time for actors for this second blessing was 5:45 am on July 11, 2011 in the new *Hawaii Five-0* headquarters (the old Advertiser Building on Kapiolani Boulevard). Sometime around 6:30 am, *Hawaii News Now* filmed Kekuna as he gathered everyone from a time of reminiscing with friends from cast and crew to join him in the pronouncement of the traditional Hawaiian blessing. Kekuna prefaced his blessing with a few words, inviting everyone to encourage one another, need one another, never take each other for granted, and forgive each other. He reminded everyone present that no one is perfect and that each has been called to this particular time and this particular place by Divine Appointment. No one else has the ability to do their job. Kekuna offered a prayer thanking God for a successful first season and asking blessings on the second. He recognized the many members of the crew who work tirelessly and thanked God for sustenance and jobs the series has made available to the people of Hawaii. He then asked O'Loughlin and Lenkov to step forward, join hands, and bow heads with everyone for a prayer blessing. Following this, he had O'Loughlin and Lenkov untie the maile lei.[6] The maile lei has a type of green, scented leaf native to the rainforests of Hawaii. It is often used at memorable or special occasions, and it has a sweet fragrance. It is also referred to as the "lei of royalty". Obviously, there has been no royalty in Hawaii for quite some time. So, today the maile lei symbolizes honoring and welcoming the Kingship of Jesus Christ. The maile lei is open ended in appearance and hangs down. It is said to bring good luck. For this occasion, O'Loughlin wore his lei threaded with Hawaiian flowers. Kekuna described the Hawaiian blessing as "basically Christian with some traditions of Hawaii thrown in." Kekuna travels worldwide to give blessings and always likes people to participate and honor God in his blessings.[7]

Kia too described the blessing as "Christian Hawaiian and culturally significant." His Season Three blessing of the series took place at Manoa Valley District Park at Waikiki Beach on July 9, 2012, and it was indeed a formal program, as all Hawaiian blessings are. "The theme of the third season was based on the concept of family; everybody taking care of family," Kia said. "So, everything at the blessing that we spoke of in Hawaiian had to reflect a concept of having a sense of family – among friends, among colleagues, among staff, among production. Although we're not blood related, we have to treat each other like family and take care of each other. That's the only way anything in life can ever be successful and achieve its goal is to really be a unit, to be a family." Unlike the previous blessings, this one was presented mostly in Hawaiian, with Kia using chants during the ceremony. "When we chant the chant of our forefathers," he says, "it's very different than just talking or saying a prayer." Kia has blessed other series through the years, including *Lost* and *Knight Rider*.[8]

The cast returned on set Wednesday, July 10, 2013 for the Season Four blessing. Prior to the blessing, stars, producers, and crew members gathered to greet each other, marking the end of a two-month hiatus for the show. Lead actor and full-bearded Alex O'Loughlin, who had literally just returned to the Island and hadn't had time to shave, revealed to *Hawaii News Now* reporter Tannya Joaquin via live stream that this was the first time he had seen the new surroundings. He expressed excitement on beginning the new season. Executive Producer/Showrunner Peter Lenkov also revealed that, contrary to rumors, Grace Park would be returning to the series. (The Season Three finale had Kono bidding everyone farewell before boarding a boat with Adam, bound for Shanghai). The blessing of the new sound stage and upcoming season consisted of prayers and chants pronounced by Kauila Kawelo Barber and Kalei Nu'uhiwa. Lenkov, along with series stars O'Loughlin and Daniel Dae Kim ended the blessing by untying the maile lei. Also in attendance were Honolulu Mayor Kirk Caldwell and series stars Michelle Borth, Dennis Chun, Teilor Grubbs, Al Harrington, and Taylor Wiley. Joaquin explained that Scott Caan and Grace Park had not yet arrived on the Island.[9] Following the pronouncement of the blessing, everyone was off to shoot the first scenes of Season Four.

The cast returned to set to shoot Season Five on July 8, 2014. O'Loughlin, Kim, and Park were in attendance, and the *Hawaii News Now* live streamed event took place in Waikiki. Kahu Kauila Kawelo Barber, Five-0 Hawaiian Language and Protocol Advisor, delivered the blessing, which focused on the number "five". Also in attendance for this blessing were Lenkov, Al Harrington and Dennis Chun. Following this very brief blessing time, cast and crew began filming the new season.[10]

Season Six's blessing found the cast and crew at Koko Head Community Park at 6:30 am on July 8, 2015. The blessing was pronounced by Kahu Kordell Kekoa, who had already appeared in the series as kahu for Chin Ho and Malia's wedding, "Alaheo Pau'ole" (Gone Forever).[11] Cast and crew present included Dennis Chun, Ian Anthony Dale, Co-Executive Producer Jeff Downer, Jorge Garcia, Daniel Dae Kim, Executive Producer Peter Lenkov, Alex O'Loughlin, Chi McBride, Grace Park, Christopher Sean, and Co-Executive Producer/Director Bryan Spicer. One unofficial cast mate present was O'Loughlin's dog, Dusty.[12]

NOW • DID YOU KNOW • DID YOU KNOW • DID YOU KNOW • DID YOU KNOW • DID YO

Actor Moe Keale (Truck Kealoha in the original Five-O*) had a great relationship with many of the Hawaiian kahuna and spiritual people. He worked with Jack Lord and others to bring people of authority into the blessings.*[13]

Production offices for the Hawaii Five-0 *reboot have been located at the Hilton Hawaiian Village (Season One), the old Advertiser Building (Season Two and Season Three), and The Hawaii Film Studio (Seasons Four, Five and Six).*

Hawaii Five-0 came home for the Season Four blessing, with the production of Season Four being on the same sound stage as the original series.[14]

At the time of the Season Five blessing, news broke that Carol Burnett would return to the series to play McGarrett's Aunt Deb.[15]

The blessings for Season One and Season Two took place at the series' Production Office locations.

Chapter 4
THE FANS

A Glimpse Behind... Sunset on the Beach

Unlike the traditional Hawaiian blessings of the series, "Sunset on the Beach" is a relatively new phenomenon. The concept was born when Jeremy Harris, former Mayor of Honolulu, decided shortly after 9/11 that the City needed some community activities to help boost its economy.

To that end, he developed a "free" weekend event with food (sold by vendors along the beach), music, and a movie on a 30-foot screen in Waikiki. Coordinator of the project, Janet Lee Maduli, recalls the unveiling of the "Sunset on the Beach" event. It took place at Kuhio Beach and featured the premiere of Edgy Lee's "Waikiki: In the Wake of Dreams". One hundred torches were lit at sunset, and entertainment was provided by Don Ho and his daughter, Hoku, along with the Royal Hawaiian Band. The event featured lei sellers, coconut huskers, and lauhala weavers.[1] Sunset on the Beach quickly became

Above: Awaiting star arrivals on the red carpet at Queen's Surf Beach (from the author's personal collection). Below: It's showtime at Sunset on the Beach (photo credit: Meryl Hollar, from the author's personal collection)

an outlet for the launching of a new TV series. In 2003, *The Ride* brought its world premiere to the event, followed by *North Shore* and *Lost* in 2004.[2]

Then came the *Hawaii Five-0* reboot and its red-carpet seasonal premieres. Prior to the debut of the reboot of the series, more than 5,000 people gathered on September 13, 2010 to meet the new cast. In attendance were series regulars Alex O'Loughlin, Scott Caan, Daniel Dae Kim, and Grace Park. Also present were Al Harrington (Det Ben Kokua in the original *Five-O* and Mamo Kahike in the reboot) and Taryn Manning (McGarrett's sister, Mary).[3] The special evening that knit together original and reboot included a touching note from James MacArthur, read by Harrington. (This note will be fully revealed in Chapter 9).[4]

Further tying the series together was an appearance by Leonard and Rose Freeman's daughters, who spoke about their father and the series and read a note from their mother, wishing the producers well. Executive Producers Peter Lenkov, Alex Kurtzman, and Roberto Orci were present, and a word was also shared on behalf of the new cast by Kim.[5] Entertainment for the evening included Willie K (with Aidan Laprete joining for some songs), Makana and Taimane Gardner, the University of Hawaii (UH) Rainbow Marching Band (which performed the *Five-O* theme), and UH's Rainbow Dancers.[6]

When the reboot was renewed for a second season, another Sunset on the Beach event was held, this time on September 10, 2011. Besides O'Loughlin, Caan, Kim, and Park, among those in attendance were Mark Dacascos (Wo Fat), Lauren German (Agent Lori Weston), Teilor Grubbs (Grace Williams), Masi Oka (Dr. Max Bergman), Terry O'Quinn (Joe White), and Taylor Wily (Kamekona). Producers Lenkov and Orci were also present. A short speech was given by CBS President, David Stapf, and Commissioner Walea Constantinau of the Honolulu Film Office had this to say, "This show is so close to the Islands and the Island people feel so close to it that this is a way for the creators and CBS to give back in the place where it is filmed and celebrate the show with everybody."[7] Nonstophonolulu.com reported that "*Hawaii Five-0* Day" was proclaimed by the Mayor of Honolulu, Peter Carlisle, and the Governor of Hawaii, Neil Abercrombie. Entertainment was provided by Hapa, and there was also fire dancing.

By the time Season Three rolled around, "The Star Advertiser" and "Honolulu Pulse," along with *Hawaii News Now* had become old pros on the red carpet As per the prior two events, a good time was had by all. O'Loughlin and Kim were on hand for this third-time event, along with Orci and Lenkov. Special guests included Nina Tassler (President of CBS Entertainment), Mayor Peter Carlisle, Governor Neil Abercrombie, Michelle Borth (Catherine Rollins), Oka, and Wily.[8] Grubbs, Harrington, and Dennis Chun (Sgt Duke Lukela) were also spotted.

It goes without saying that all three events ended with a screening of the new season's premiere on the 30-foot screen on that portion of Waikiki known as Queen's Surf Beach. September 26, 2013 likewise heralded in Season Four with the Jonas Brothers performing. Making appearances and chatting with the

Below: The sun sets on Queens Surf Beach, Sunset on the Beach, 2012 (from the author's personal collection). Right: Alex O'Loughlin at Sunset on the Beach red carpet (photo credit: Meryl Hollar, from the author's personal collection)

press were Alex Kurtzman, Peter Lenkov, Alex O'Loughlin, Daniel Dae Kim, Michelle Borth, Al Harrington, Mark Dacascos, Masi Oka, and new series regular Chi McBride. An introduction to Season Five and the upcoming 100th episode of the series[9] took place on September 13, 2014, with Grace Park also putting in an appearance and Jorge Garcia making his debut as series regular. Season Six's Sunset on the Beach took place on September 12, 2015 with the usual cast and crew attendees, including Grace Park. Visibly absent were Alex Kurtzman and Roberto Orci.

"Sunset on the Beach" Back in the Day

O bviously, there was no such thing as a "Sunset on the Beach" back in the day of the original *Five-O,* but there was plenty of pomp and circumstance. Margaret Doversola, Jack Lord's Personal Assistant, noted that, prior to each season's premiere, there was an invitation-only press dinner on Oahu, where Lord formally "introduced" each new season to the press. Over the years, this dinner was held in various places on Oahu, most notably in Kahala, where Lord owned a condo. The dinner also served as a sort of introduction of Jack Lord, the actor, to new press. Lord also took this opportunity to present gifts of appreciation to both cast and crew.[10] (More stories about these press dinners will be revealed in Chapter 10).

W • DID YOU KNOW • DID YOU KNOW • DID YOU KNOW • DID YOU KNOW • DID YOU I

Margaret Doversola worked as Jack Lord's Personal Assistant for the last five years of the series and continued to work for him in this capacity for the remainder of his life. She is now a well-known casting director in Honolulu who can regularly be seen giving lectures and teaching acting around the Hawaiian Islands.[11]

An unofficial online Hawaii Five-O fan club was established for the original series. It ran for many years after the series left the air. According to information there, prior to the original series' premiere on the small screen, there was an invitation-only black-tie World Premiere event at a New York City theatre.[12]

Daniel Dae Kim also made appearances on the Waikiki Sunset on the Beach red carpet as a star of ABC-TV's Lost. [14]

THE DIRECTORS

Time Out for an Episodic Glimpse... The Directors

Just as many sunsets and dinners for seasonal premieres of Five-O have come and gone, so have many directors. Directors of the original *Hawaii Five-O* series over the years were Edward M. Abroms, Corey Allen, Danny Arnold, Abner Biberman, Bruce Bilson, Barry Crane, Herschel Daugherty, Dennis Donnelly, Harry Falk, David Friedkin, Harry Harris, Gordon Hessler, Herbert Hirschman, Alf Kjellin, Anton Leader, Bernard McEveety, Irving J. Moore, Gene Nelson, Ernest Pintoff, Allen Reisner, Jack Shea, Barry Shear, Bob Sweeney, and Don Weis.[1] Only four are still living, or at least not confirmed otherwise, at press time (Edward M. Abroms, Bruce Bilson, Dennis Donnelly, and Harry Falk). Jack Lord, who by most word-of-mouth accounts from those who either knew him or worked with him, maintained much of the creative control of *Hawaii Five-O* following Leonard Freeman's passing, directed six episodes of the original series himself. Those episodes were "Death with Father" (airdate January 22, 1974), "How to Steal a Masterpiece" (November 12, 1974), "Honor Is an Unmarked Grave" (November 28, 1975), "The Bells Toll at Noon" (January 6, 1977), "Why Won't Linda Die?" (December 14, 1978), and "Who Says Cops Don't Cry?" (October 11, 1979).[2]

Directors of the *Five-0* reboot have included Matt Earl Beesley, Steve Boyum, Jeff Cadiente, Duane Clark, Joe Dante, Steven DePaul, Paul A. Edwards, Chris Fisher, Gwyneth Horder-Playton, Jeffrey Hunt, Elodie Keene, Eric Laneuville, Jerry Levine, Allison Liddi-Brown, Christine Moore, Bryan Spicer, Brad Tanenbaum, Larry Teng, Jeff T. Thomas, Frederick E. O. Toye, Brad Turner, Maja Vrvilo, Peter Weller, Sylvain White, James Whitmore, Jr. , Len Wiseman, Kate Woods, and Alex Zakrzewski.[3] In Season Five, Daniel Dae Kim even took a turn at directing with "Kuka'awale," Stakeout (February 27, 2015).

A few "dissected" *Five-0* episodes from the first few seasons offer interesting personal viewpoints in the words of Boyum[4] and Dante[5]:

Title: "Ha'i'ole" (Unbreakable)
In the Words of Director: Steve Boyum
Original Air Date: September 19, 2011
This was the premiere of Season Two, and the author's favorite episode of the series to date.

Boyum: "That was a big one. One of the challenges was just the physical aspect of having McGarrett (O'Loughlin) in a wife-beater tank top and having him just jump out of an ambulance at 25 miles per hour. Jeff Cadiente, Stunt Coordinator, and I came up with the idea of putting a wet suit on him. Otherwise, you could imagine the road rash. Alex did part of that stunt himself. Obviously, he has a stunt double, Justin Sundquist. But, Alex generally is very active in doing a

Steve Boyum (photo courtesy of Steve Boyum)

lot of his own stunts. He's a martial artist and really a physical guy, so if you let him, he'll do most anything. But, he relied on Justin to do this one. And Justin's one of the best young stunt guys in the business. One thing that I thought was one of the neatest things about that whole episode was the amount of time that there's no dialogue, from the time Alex is in the ambulance to when he's in the bathroom - five minutes. For television, that's unheard of, and to carry that much intensity is really unheard of. That nobody thought to loop a line in there, I thought, was a testament to Al (Alex). I take a little credit for figuring out a way to shoot it. It was a big, big episode. It was a great script. Peter wrote that, and most of the scripts he writes are very, very good. They wrote a huge episode for the finale of that season as well."

> I've wanted to direct since I was a kid. Basically, as a Director, you try to bring to life what the writers of a series write. You anticipate what the camera needs to see. And the writers in *Five-0* are always really ambitious. What they write is sometimes really the impossible. A lot of people are afraid to admit some things are too overwhelming to direct. But, we Directors have to figure out how to shoot an episode in like nine days.
> *Steve Boyum*

Title: "Ma'ema'e'" (Clean)
Director: Steve Boyum
Original Air Date: October 17, 2011
Boyum: "This was one of the harder ones, and it's one of my favorites. It was a phenomenal script, written by Stephanie Sengupta. That one was really a labor of love. At the end of the day, I really was very pleased with it. Grace (Park) was great on the final act. And we had wonderful cooperation with the bank we used. They let us actually go down into the vault. We did that one on a weekend as well. They also let us shoot in the lobby."

Title: "Ka Iwi kapu" (Sacred Bones)
In the Words of Director: Joe Dante
Original Airdate: October 31, 2011
Dante; "The remarkable thing about this episode is that they've been extremely clever in how much of Hawaiian lore they've incorporated into the show. There's a lot of attention paid to customs and the personalities and of Hawaii being a distinct society."

Title: "Kupale" (Defender)
Director: Steve Boyum
Original Air Date: February 20, 2012

Boyum: "I really loved this episode with the Koa warriors and the coin. It was a really cool challenge and one that I had to get technically correct or we would have gotten thrown off the Island for sure. Shooting about the Hawaiian culture *is* a lot of fun. I worked with Blaine, *Five-0's* Hawaiian Cultural Advisor, on the Koa warrior sequence. It was nice to be able to tell a Hawaiian story there."

Title: "Ua Hala" (Death in the Family)
Director: Steve Boyum
Original Air Date: May 14, 2012

About this season finale, Boyum said, "It's almost easier to do a season opener, even though you always want to come in and go out with a bang. Most series, by the time you've done 23-24 episodes, you've pretty much broken the bank. Your financials are pretty much on the downward side when you're doing a seasonal finale. Anyway, we still spent good money on the finale. One of the challenges on that one was to find a building we could blow up. We scoured the City of Honolulu to find something. Then, Jeff Downer came up with the idea of using the front of our Production Offices at the old Advertiser Building.

"So, what we had to do was shoot on a Sunday, and we had to do it before 11:00 in the morning. The powers that be wanted to make this a big deal, so we had to shut down the street that building happens to be on, which is Kapiolani Boulevard, a main drag in Honolulu. And we had to re-route traffic. Then, there was a shoot-out at the end of that episode at the pet clinic. I wanted this to be technically correct, yet exciting. I wanted to give a 'Heat' factor to it. And that wasn't easy. If you go in and count the edits, there are quite a few. You also have to remember, we had eight days, nine days tops, to do this episode. When we did the assault on the pet clinic, I worked closely, as I did all year long, with our SEAL technical advisor, Gary Fritts.

I've learned a lot from Gary. And, after a season of working with him, at times disagreeing with him about maintaining technical reality versus dramatic license for cool factor, we were finally coming to a place where I felt that if I went to him with what I wanted to do, he and I could work it out together so that it could be technically correct, yet still exciting to the audience. Sometimes, those two things don't meet up. Gary and I planned the assault together, and when we cut the first shot of the sequence, he looked at me, and said, 'That's the coolest tactical shot I've seen in a movie.' And I thought, 'ok, we've hit the mark. Gary's happy. I'm happy. We'll print that shot, and we'll move on to the next.' That's the way we did that whole assault. Technically, it's really accurate, and it's exciting as well."

Title: "Lana I Ka Moana" (Adrift)
Director: Steve Boyum
Original Air Date: October 8, 2012

Boyum: "I think this was the single most challenging episode with the series, and one of the most difficult I've ever done in my career, including work with feature films I've been involved with. We had four days to shoot basically everything that was on the water. And that included when Daniel Dae, Grace, and Michelle Borth find the boat in the marina. That part alone took about three hours. We had to do it rather quickly, because we were on a dock. What happens when you're out in the ocean, though, is that nothing stays in one place. The hurdles for shooting are immense. First of all, the scene that takes place is in chronological time… Let's say one scene is five minutes of dialogue. Over the course of the amount of time it takes to film that dialogue, the ocean conditions and wind are changing. All you can do is hope that the sea conditions match when you do a close-up of Danny and a close-up of McGarrett, and it's a reverse angle. You have to be sure it's not glassy on one side and windy on the other. Imagine you've got a crew of over 90 people, cast and crew, that you have to have out in the ocean, and you've got them in a flotilla of vessels. And, you're gonna shoot from one boat to another. You've got currents; you've got wind. You've got land that's gonna come into frame eventually. Then, everything starts to drift around in circles 'cuz the wind's blowing it. Michael Newman, the AD on that episode, by the way, is one of the best AD's I've ever worked with.

"I storyboarded that entire scene, drew all the panels. The AD, my cameraman Alan Caso, and I spent four days of our prep time, which is seven days basically, lining up storyboards. Chronologically, over the course of the day, we might shoot two different scenes, broken up into what we call block shooting. You want to put Alex and Scott in a situation where they can stay in the moment. Alex and Scott are really great at doing that, by the way. When we have to shoot out of order and do all close-ups one way and then all close-ups the other, they're so good at that. All of the cast is really. They've gotten very good at being able to get back to where they were two scenes ago. And they really held it together during the course of four days. Anyway, we were shooting just on the west side of the Island. Trade winds blow land to sea generally only a mile off shore. If the trade winds blow 20-25 mph, it's pretty smooth. But, if the winds blow what they call 'Kona,' which is from the south, the water gets really choppy. So, over the course of four days, we had to roll the dice that we got some consistent weather, that it wouldn't rain one day and not another. Needless to say, we spent about four days just planning shot for shot, hoping we'd get out there what we had on our wish list. So, we had plan A, B, and C, trying to cover all the contingencies we could. But, we couldn't anticipate everything. We had one day when the wind changed about four o'clock, and the chop came in. We got knocked all over the place. The clouds came in, and we got so miserable, we had to wrap early. That meant we lost two hours of shooting. It also meant the next day, we had to shoot 11 pages of work. That was a nightmare, I gotta tell you. In the end, if we had not planned it the way we did, we never would have gotten it. And that's a testament to the crew. The *Five-0* crew is one of the best crews I've ever worked with, from the camera guys to the grips to the electricians. Eighty percent of the shooting crew are local to Hawaii, having grown up there or lived there a long time, so they're used to working in and out of the water. We got through that one unscathed. That was a very difficult episode. In addition, we usually have one day for every episode where we have a second unit. That one we did with just one crew, in eight days. I couldn't do that with a lot of crews. That was a 'hats off' to everybody on the show, including the actors. Both of them (O'Loughlin and Caan) only got mad at me once or twice in four days. I'm like their stepfather. They'll lash out at me before they will someone else. We're like family. Come to think of it, I also had to have Daniel Dae hang off a building in that episode."

Title: "Olelo Pa'a" (The Promise)
Director: Joe Dante
Original Air Date: April 15, 2013
(Hawaii doubling again as North Korea)
Dante: "It was a leap of faith to say, 'okay, we'll try to make Hawaii look like Korea'. It's a little too verdant. When I was growing up, war movies I saw were shot in the Hollywood Hills, where there were no trees. It's like when you go to Canada. You want to make everything look like New York City, but it doesn't. It looks like Canada. It's just something you have to live with. We did try to take out some of the color, though, to try to make it not look so much like Hawaii."

Directing the episode proved challenging for Dante in more than one way. For one thing, it took a left turn from the normal "procedural" theme, focusing more on McGarrett. Most of those scenes that were cut were where Danno and the other members of the team were trying to find out where McGarrett was.

Joe Dante (photo courtesy of Joe Dante and Mark Alan, Renfield Productions)

Dante: "There's a scene with Terry O'Quinn on a horse that was followed by O'Quinn at this Montana cabin (Hawaii doubling as Montana, of course), where they're trying to get him to tell them where McGarrett is. Of course, he won't. And there's another scene with Jimmy Buffett at the bar where he gets a phone call from Danno, and he gives him the runaround, and won't tell him where McGarrett is. This is an attempt to keep the other characters alive during the show. I knew when I was shooting it that this was the first material that was gonna have to go, because it wasn't anything to do with the plot at all. And when I handed in my cut, I left those things out. And I didn't expect them to be put back, and they weren't."

Even so, Dante spent an entire day with Caan, Kim, and Park, shooting those scenes that never made it on screen.

Another "cut" that never made it was "a brief scene of McGarrett and Catherine putting the body in a truck before they leave the hand grenade under the bad guy (played by Rick Yune). This didn't really tell you anything important, other than that they moved the body and that it was obviously going to go somewhere else. As far as the actual mechanics of how they did that, it's just one of those things where you can't get into that level of detail unless you want it to be a two-parter. The challenge really was that it was a big episode to try to fit into our day-to-day schedule," though it did fit into the requisite eight-day, or nine-day, shooting schedule. Location proved to be somewhat of a concern. "We had a lot of locations that took a long time to get to. And then once you shot there, you had to go home, and then you had to come back. The days were a little longer than usual. Also, you try to work these things out so that everything is nearby itself. Once you go to the trouble to get there, you can actually shoot a lot of different things in the area, which we were able to do. We were on somebody's ranch and luckily, the entire compound for the bad guys, the initial landing, and all those things could all be done in that same place. Unfortunately, it was on the other side of the Island. And there's no place to stay. You can't say, 'I'll just stay in a motel.' You can only be picked up and taken there.

"Then there's the fact that Alex, who's the lead of the show of course, had to get a haircut to be a Navy SEAL. So, in the middle of the production, he went and got a buzz cut. Because of logistics of availability of actors and things like that, there was just no way to schedule it so that he could do it at the end of the shoot. The problem was, there were still things left to shoot with his old hair. And that meant that he had to wear a wig, which was very uncomfortable for him to have to do. Then, there were certain actors available only on certain days. Terry O'Quinn arrived from the East Coast on the day he was to shoot. He was late because of some screw-up, so you're constantly juggling what's possible in the time that you have. I'm happy that it turned out as well as it did. Part of that is due to Alex, who took this episode very, very seriously. He's very tight with the Navy SEAL community, so he really wanted it to be a good episode. And he came up with a lot of ideas, many of which we used. We also had military advisors. You would think that they'd be intrusive in the scene, that you'd set up something and then they'd come to you and say, 'you know that's not really the way we do it.' But in this case, it was actually very beneficial. They were tremendously helpful. The guys in the mock Navy SEAL training on the beach were the real deal. We looked at a lot of photos of stuff, of how it's done. But you really don't know until you do it how dangerous it really is, particularly in Hawaii, with the riptides. You can easily be taken out to sea. All of our extras were real Navy guys. Because the *Hawaii Five-0* group is so connected to that community, we were able to get a lot of help from those guys. A real Chaplain delivered the eulogy in the funeral scene. We had real Officers in speaking parts. The 21-gun salute guys were the real deal. And they were all doing it by the book. I had no idea how they actually worked until the day I showed up. I just said, 'Let's just do it in real time and shoot it in real time.' So we did the entire ceremony, which took about 16-17 minutes. It's all very ritualized. They even salute in slow motion. But, in the end, the editors (Supervising Editor, Maja Vrvilo) did a remarkable job condensing it without losing anything. All of the pomp and circumstance and stuff, it's all there. And it's even kind of moving. They managed to edit it all around the folding of the flag, which takes about nine times longer than it did on the show. Nonetheless, you still get the impression, and it worked out very well. Another problem was the little girl (played by Mykayla Sohn). We shot two 18-minute takes in real time without being able to see how it looked. By the time it came around to doing the stuff on the little girl, she was so fidgety and so bored that she was constantly talking and walking away, losing interest beyond belief. And here's Alex. He's in this big scene with this kid who is babbling at him. But, we managed to figure out a way to do it. The editors (led by Vrvilo) found the right pieces. But, it was challenging."

And about those ideas from O'Loughlin, who, according to Dante, has a bit of a reputation for being somewhat of a perfectionist when it comes to his thoughts on the episodes

Another issue on this show, on almost all TV shows, is that, since they're run by writers, often the scripts are longer than there is time on the show. There's only 41 minutes, or 42 minutes, of show. The rest of it is commercials. So, you know going in that you're shooting things that aren't going to be in the show. And that's always a little frustrating about television, because the better part of the day doesn't get into the show. And, it's not just this show. It's almost every show. It's really being able to present the images in a way that makes sense to you and that is in keeping with the general intent of the show. You can have some freedom with the guest stars for one or two episodes, but for the most part, the lead actors already know how to play their parts, and they've been playing them quite successfully before you get there.

Joe Dante

… the Director said, "He's very good about it. It was his idea to come into the scene of the Officers' tent wearing combats. He thought he should come in wearing fatigues, covered in dirt, as if he'd just gotten off a plane out in the desert. And it was a good idea. It was one of those last-minute things where it's such a good idea that you have to make time to do it. But Alex really liked this episode."

Dante was especially proud of the rapport established between O'Loughlin and Alan Ritchson (Freddie Hart) as training buddies. "Ritchson was really a good choice, but all the material we saw on him that got him the job was all completely disbarred from the character he played. It was all comedy stuff, and it was very broad. But it was just something that made us think. And he turned out to be really good in the role. They complemented each other and made a very believable duo. I think that's really the soul of the show. O'Loughlin, of course, did not do the HALO jump, but he does do most of his stunts. In this particular episode, he did everything except stop Ritchson from ringing the bell and knocking down the Korean combatant as McGarrett and Hart were fleeing the enemy camp. Those were stunt guys, but he did everything else himself."

Dante found some location shoots for this episode particularly interesting. The hangar where the coffin was, for instance, was actually involved in the initial Pearl Harbor raid. "There are bullet holes throughout the entire building. So, it's really kinda cool to be in that building and soak up that history." In the end, Dante surmised that "the locations are really what you make them. One thing we did compromise on was the barracks. There were much better barracks, but, again, they were too far away. Also, the Officers' headquarters was a second choice. But, we made it work." Another thing they made work was the rain – and the mud. So much mud! "The funny thing is, it rained constantly throughout the entire episode, especially for the opening scene at the handoff at the Korean gate. I had mud in my shoes when I came home, complete and utter mud. And, there was all this rain, all the time, at the location with the Korean compound. Sometimes, it was raining in the shots. But the mud was just unbelievable."

In the end, Dante and crew pulled it off. But, he admitted to having second thoughts in the beginning about actually managing to pull it off. "It seemed to have the depth of a movie in it. So much stuff was happening in so many different places and with so many characters. I thought, 'are you sure we can do this in eight days?' But, we did. We actually did it in seven and a quarter if you take out the stuff we didn't use."

Dante went on to direct episodes in Season Five[6] and Season Six.[7]

NOW • DID YOU KNOW • DID YOU KNOW • DID YOU KNOW • DID YOU KNOW • DID YO

Steve Boyum began working on Hawaii Five-0 *as Guest Director on Season One, Episode 23, "Ua Hiki Mai Kapalena Pau" (Until the End Is Near). When Peter Lenkov saw the episode, he offered him a producing gig on* Five-0. *At the time, he was under contract with Warner Brothers to do another season of* Human Target. *When* Human Target *was cancelled, Boyum came to* Five-0.

The Five-0 *episode Boyum considered the most fun he produced was "Ki'ilua" (Deceiver). With the helicopters and action scenes, he considers it the best* Five-0 *episode ever done.*

Prior to directing an episode of Hawaii Five-0, *Joe Dante worked with Peter Lenkov on a Halloween episode of* CSI:NY.

Joe Dante had never worked with Robert Englund until the Halloween 2011 episode of Hawaii Five-0, *even though both film horror-genre projects, and he hopes to work with Englund on a future film project.*

Joe Dante thinks Alex O'Loughlin and Scott Caan are fun to watch, because they spark each other, even when only delivering exposition.

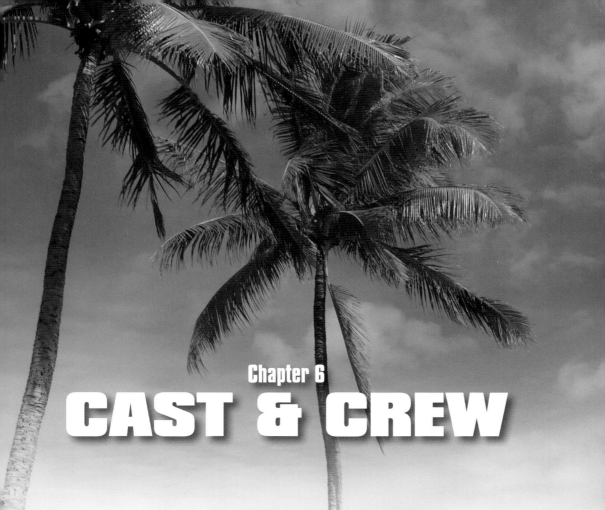

Chapter 6
CAST & CREW

A Glimpse at... Producers, Writers, Crew, and Oh, Yes, Recurring Characters

Directors are not the only "necessities" of a television production. Producers, writers, crew, and recurring characters are all vital to the success of a series like *Hawaii Five-0,* and they all work together in their area of expertise to bring a finely tuned finished product to the small screen.

Every member of the team is important – and necessary – to the success or failure of the series. Crewmembers are treasures, and their jobs seem endless. Margaret Doversola was one of the invaluable crewmembers of the original *Five-O.* (Look for a story or two about her boss in Chapter 10). Doversola's main job in the beginning was doing script changes. She explains, "I answered the phones, typed and dictated letters, and did script changes. I used to do those changes when there was nothing but hearing it on the phone and typing it up. There were no computers or faxes. I had to xerox each page, one at a time, collate them myself, fold them, and give them out. It's just like today, only without electronics. It was a lot of hard work, a lot of overtime, and a lot of stress. But, I really enjoyed my job, and I learned everything from helping the writers and Producers to being in the Production Office for awhile. I think I did everything but camera and sound work."[1] Doversola also cast the pilot of the *Five-0* reboot, hiring 11 actors and all the extras.

The series would not exist without cast – or writers. Writers of the original series included Leonard Freeman, Jerome Coopersmith, Bill Stratton, Robert James, Mel Goldberg, Jerrold L. Ludwig, Eric Bercovici, Alvin Sapinsley, and John D.F. Black.[2] Writers of the reboot to date have included Alex Kurtzman, Peter M. Lenkov, Roberto Orci, Leonard Freeman (credited), Carol Barbee, Tara Butters, Sarah Byrd, Travis Donnelly, John Dove, Michele Fazekas, Jim Galasso, Melissa Glenn, Sarah Goldfinger, Jessica Granger, Eric Guggenheim, Joe Halpin, Kyle Harimoto, Bill Haynes, Christina M. Kim, Moira Kirland, Kenny Kyle, Steven Lillien, Akeba Gaddis Lynn, Lorenzo Manetti, Noah Nelson, Sue Palmer, Bradley Paul, Elwood Reid, Jessica Rieder, Mike Schaub, Shane Salerno, Stephanie Sengupta, Ken Solarz, Peter M. Tassler, Matt Wheeler, David Wolkove, Bryan Wynbrandt, and Paul Zbyszewski.[3] Producers, crew, writers… *Hawaii Five-0* (original and reboot) would not be in production if it weren't for any of these talented people. The Production would also not be the same without its recurring characters.

In the original *Hawaii Five-O*, the same actor would return to the series over a period of time and play a different role in each episode in which he appeared.[4] For example, "KeAloha" Rodney Philip Aiu (Rod Aiu) appeared in nine segments of the original series and played a different character in each episode. Unfortunately, he was – and is - known as the guy who killed Chin Ho Kelly. That episode, "A Death in the Family," aired in 1978. Other segments in which Aiu guest starred were "Requiem for a Saddle Bronc Rider (1977), "The Cop on the Cover" (1977), "Ready, Aim…" (1977), "A Short Walk on the Long Shore" (1978), "A Long Time Ago" (1978, credited as Christerpher Neddels), "The Executive File" (1979), "The Flight of the Jewels" (1980 – original title "Her Majesty's Jewels"), and "The Moroville Coveant" (1980, credited as Christerpher Neddels). Interestingly, Aiu had many unsuccessful reads for *Five-0* for years before he was cast in a role. Whenever he auditioned, he always competed against the same actors.[5] Fortunately, Location Casting Director Richard Kindelon seemed to sympathize with him. Kindelon gave Aiu a bit of "friendly advice." He said, "Next time you read for a part, just be yourself. Don't pretend to be anybody else." The advice worked, and the next time Aiu had an opportunity to read for the Producers, he got the part.[6] (Be on the lookout for an amusing story from Aiu about Jack Lord in Chapter

Above: Michelle Borth (photo credit: Meryl Hollar, from the author's personal collection). Below: Ian Anthony Dale (photo credit: Meryl Hollar, from the author's personal collection)

10). Then, there was Moe Keale, who was actually coached into acting by Jack Lord and ended up with a regular role in the final season of the original series.[7] He and his wife became close friends with Jack and Marie Lord, and his story is told in Chapter 10. He apparently played many roles from 1971-1978, then took the role of Detective Truck Kealoha for the final season. Glenn Cannon, Professor at the University of Hawaii at Manoa, had a recurring role as District

Attorney in the original *Five-O*. Sadly, he passed away as this book was being written. Other actors in regular recurring roles in the original series included Khigh Dheigh (Wo Fat), Richard Denning (Governor Paul Jameson), and Herman

Wedemeyer (Sgt. Duke Lukela). Herman Wedemeyer and Al Harrington (Ben Kokua) both had several roles in different episodes of the original *Five-O* before being cast as "Duke" and "Ben," respectively.[8]

In the *Hawaii Five-0* reboot, actors playing recurring roles or recurring cast have included Kala Alexander (Kawika), Reiko Aylesworth (Malia Waincroft), William Baldwin (Frank Delano), Michelle Borth (Lt. Catherine Rollins, who was added as a series regular in Season Three, then dropped for Season Five and Season Six), Jimmy Buffett (Frank Bama), Carol Burnett (Aunt Deb), Dennis Chun (Sgt. Duke Lukela), Ian Anthony Dale (Adam Noshimuri), Mark Deklin (Stan Edwards), Mirrah Foulkes (Ellie Clayton), Jorge Garcia (Jerry Ortega, who was added as a series regular in Season Five), Lauren German (Lori Weston), Melanie Griffith (Clara Williams), Teilor Grubbs (Grace Williams), Daniel Henney (Michael Noshimuri), Kelly Hu (Laura Hills), Richard T. Jones (Gov. Sam Denning), David Keith (Wade Gutches), Christine Lahti (Doris McGarrett), Will Yun Lee (Sang Min), Larry Manetti (Nicky "The Kid" Demarco),

Top: Chi McBride (photo credit: Meryl Hollar, from the author's personal collection). Center: Taryn Manning (photo courtesy of Much and House Public Relations). Bottom: Mark Dacascos (photo credit: Wade Brands, photo courtesy of Mary Putnam Greene)

Chapter 6 – CAST & CREW

James Marsters (Victor Hesse), Chi McBride (Lou Grover, who was added as a series regular in Season Four), Masi Oka (Dr. Max Bergman, who was added as a series regular in Season Two), Larisa Oleynik (Jenna Kaye), Terry O'Quinn (Joe White), Lindsay Price (Leilani), Autumn Reeser (Gabby Asano), William Sadler (John McGarrett), Christopher Sean (Gabriel Waincroft), Lili Simmons (Amber Vitale), Tom Sizemore (Vince Fryer), Jean Smart (Gov. Pat Jameson), Martin Starr (Adam "Toast" Charles), Shawn Anthony Thomsen (Officer Pua Kai), Claire van der Boom (Rachel), Taylor Wiley (Kamekona), the late Keo Woolford (Det. James Chang), and Brian Yang (Dr. Charlie Fong). But there's one actor who stands out as the only actor to have regular roles in both original and reboot series of *Hawaii Five-0*. That actor is Al Harrington, who played lead character Ben Kokua in the original series and who plays Mamo Kahike in the reboot. Chapter 7 honors his work as Kokua. And the part of Mamo was written specifically for Harrington by Peter Lenkov as part of the McGarrett "family." Mamo, in fact, taught McGarrett how to surf and had a distinct part in his growing up years. Two other recurring actors from the *Five-0* reboot are Taryn Manning (Mary McGarrett, Steve's sister) and Mark Dacascos (Wo Fat).

Manning, an accomplished singer way before *Five-0,* desperately wanted to play the role of Mary.[9] She explains, "I put myself on tape and sent it in. The network watched my tape, and I got the part. I connect my life to each experience and really round out the character." One scene, in particular, really spoke to Manning. It was filmed just after the death of her father. In the scene, Mary sat beside her father's grave and spoke to him. Manning confided that, there were a lot of authentic emotions pouring out of her.[10] Though her storyline is a side story, and though she is not one of the members of Five-0, Manning admits that she loves the show, and she loves Hawaii. She usually knows about a month ahead of time when her character will recur and makes herself available to the producers to play the part. She has even been known to pass on film roles to play the part of Mary. "It's the hardest part I've ever played," she confides. "One season, Mary was a flight attendant. I think that would have been funny to develop. But, when the next script arrived, Mary wasn't a flight attendant anymore. I thought, 'This girl's really unpredictable.' She's just an individual finding herself. And, she loves her brother very much. I see them getting closer. I'd love to see them get even closer and have more time together, one on one. It'd be interesting to watch their relationship evolve. And, the fans like to see McGarrett with his sister. They wait for us when we're on. They get to see his softer side. And I know we will have that relationship as long as the show is on." Besides loving acting in *Five-0,* Manning loves animals and doing what she can to help others. Her work with the homeless shelter and the animal shelter are two of the most important projects in her life. She also stars in the Netflix series *Orange is the New Black.*

McGarrett's archenemy Wo Fat was killed by McGarrett in the series' 100th episode, which aired in Season Five.[11] Mark Dacascos[12] was ecstatic when he was offered the role of Wo Fat. Speaking in an interview prior to the knowledge of his character's demise, Dacascos was candid. "Years ago, I did a TV series called *The Crow, Stairway to Heaven* and Peter Lenkov was one of the writers. I'm not sure what his actual process was, but on my part, basically I was out in New York doing some work, and I got this phone call from my then agent. My agent said that *Hawaii Five-0* had called and was interested in me playing the part of Wo Fat. I knew the show was up and running and the reboot, I think at that point, they had just aired a couple of episodes in the first season. They were looking at Wo Fat coming in on the twelfth or thirteenth episode. Anyway, I was aware of the show and was a fan of the original show and was ecstatic. Then, I had a conversation with Mr. Lenkov, whom I hadn't spoken with since *The Crow,* and he said 'yes,' he'd be real excited to have me as the lead villain. Of course, I was very honored and happy and accepted right away." Dacascos hails from Hawaii and remembers watching the original series with his grandparents when he was about five or six. Though he was (and still is) a huge fan of the original show, he does not get his inspiration for playing the character from the first *Five-O.* "The Wo Fat that I'm doing is based off the material and the relationship Wo Fat has with Steve McGarrett and with Doris McGarrett. I'm building his character off that and the way the actors are playing their characters in relationship to that. As an actor, I would love for the show to go a little deeper into Wo Fat's story. I know he comes from a military intelligence background. He also once worked with the CIA. But, what we see is just a moment in his life. We don't see him before a scene or after. He comes. He does some action, some intensity, and then he's out. But, as far as I'm concerned, he's got these private moments which, so far, we haven't really seen, but they're there. I do watch the show with my family, and my question is – as a fan of the show – what turned Wo Fat bad? Why was his father killed? I would love to see the 'before' Wo Fat to understand what got him to make that switch." Besides his work on *Five-0,* Dacascos has quite an impressive acting background, which includes work in the family-film project *The Lost Medallion.* In the film, some foster children find a lost medallion and learn how much

God truly loves them. Dacascos plays the role of the evil King Cobra, who he describes as "Wo Fat in the past."

Besides being an actor, Moe Keale was an accomplished Hawaiian musician.[13]

Dennis Chun is the son of actor Kam Fong (Chin Ho in the original series). Chun appeared in three different episodes of the original Five-O *as different characters.*[14]

Actor Doug Mossman had several roles in more than 25 episodes of the original series, and has also appeared one time in the reboot series, in Season Two, Episode 10, "Ki'ilua" (Deceiver).[15]

Moe Keale was honored as a living treasure a few years ago by the Sheraton Hotel as their first inductee into the Hall of Fame. He was also honored with a testament signed by every Senator from the United States Congress as well as officials of the State of Hawaii.[16]

Chi McBride's (Captain Lou Grover) character is based on a character from the original series with the same name.[17]

Ed Asner had a recurring role as August March on two episodes of the Hawaii Five-0 *reboot before his character was killed off the series. Asner had played the character of August March 37 years earlier in the original* Hawaii Five-O.[18]

Chef Masaharu Morimoto of The Modern Honolulu's Morimoto Waikiki has appeared in several Hawaii Five-0 *episodes.*[19]

Chapter 7
KONO

A Glimpse into the Lives of... Zulu and Al Harrington, True Sons of Hawaii

From its start, *Hawaii Five-O* has been about the Islands, their beauty, their location, and their people. Sunsets on the Beach, press dinners, traditional Hawaiian blessings, directors, producers, recurring characters, crew – all work together to present a package of talent and gifts that would not be complete without one more group. That group is the cast. In 1968, *Hawaii Five-O* premiered with the cast of Jack Lord, Tim O'Kelly (James MacArthur after the pilot), Kam Fong, and Zulu (Al Harrington beginning in the fifth season); in 2010, the reboot of the series premiered with the cast of Alex O'Loughlin, Scott Caan, Daniel Dae Kim, and Grace Park.

The remaining chapters of this book will concentrate on the lead actors of both the original and reboot series....

Left: Zulu in later years (photo credit: Jerry Pickard). Right: Zulu (photo credit: Jerry Pickard)

Gilbert Francis Lani Damian Kauhi (Zulu) played the role of Kono Kalakaua in the first four seasons of the original *Hawaii Five-O* (from 1968-1972). According to his biography at The Internet Movie Database, Zulu launched a successful career in stand-up comedy after leaving the show.[1] Though, sadly, he passed away in 2004, he is still fondly remembered by his friends. One of those friends is Jerry Pickard. Pickard had the privilege to get to know Zulu through interviewing him and spending time with him. Their first meeting took place at the Mahalo Con[2] in 1996. This was followed by visits with Zulu in Hilo, Hawaii in 2002 and at the Hawaii International Film Festival in November, 2003.[3] Pickard also visited Zulu at St. Francis Medical Center in Honolulu when he (Zulu) was undergoing dialysis following an unsuccessful kidney transplant. Pickard communicated via email:

"Based on our various times together, I found Zulu very outgoing, jocular, and friendly. It's fair to say he kept his beach boyishness pretty much throughout his time on earth. For example, he was prone to clown around, compassionate, wise in the ways of the world, and very aware and proud of his unique, Hawaiian heritage. He realized later in life that he'd unknowingly been an exceptional role model of sorts to his younger 'Kanaka'[4] generation, when he'd earned and initially retained the Kono part. Zulu got the role on *Five-O* when he received an invitation to a 'cattle call' casting session where he was asked to 'consume a large sandwich and bountiful beverage.' After observing this, Leonard Freeman reportedly said, 'Hey, that's it! You're going to be my Kono.' When Zulu left the series after four seasons, Freeman told him he had played the role exactly as it was meant to be played."[5] There's no clear answer as to why he left the series after four seasons, but Pickard suspects that the often heated "tete-a-tete" between Zulu and Jack Lord may have contributed largely to the reason he left. "Their personalities were direct

Al and Rosa Harrington with Meryl Hollar (left) and Cheryl Hollar (from the author's personal collection)

opposites, although both were well-meaning in their own right. Zulu was often seen as very quick to speak his mind, with a 'devil-may-care' approach which he practiced most, if not all, of his life. He felt on numerous occasions that he was not granted the respect which came with his role as Kono. For example, he was compelled to wear obviously baggy clothing, to reinforce his almost stooge-like image as envisioned by Jack Lord. Plus, the fact that Lord overtly wished to 'reign supreme' as the one and only true 'star of *Five-O*' was, in the end, unacceptably irksome to Zulu. And when Zulu did land his lucrative headliner contracts (at first with C'est Si Bon Supper Club at the Pagoda Hotel and then later at Duke's Nightclub in Waikiki), I think he likely believed he didn't need *Five-O* and the associated hassle so much."[6]

After his days on *Five-O,* he became an honorary Chairperson for the American Cancer Society of Hawaii and served in this capacity for two years. He was able to help raise over $200,000 for the cause. Pickard continues to cherish the memories of his times with Zulu "with gratitude as well as tremendous respect for a special person of Hawaiian ancestry and 'pono.'"[7] Zulu made numerous contributions to advancing the Islands and their native peoples. Pickard will never forget Zulu's inspiring bravery as personally witnessed during one of his many dialysis sessions at St. Francis. "He was a true 'Son of Hawaii' and sadly, we may never know anyone quite like him again."[8]

In the fifth season of *Hawaii Five-O,* Al Harrington was cast in the role of Ben Kokua. Harrington continued in this role until the series ended in 1980. Not an unknown to *Hawaii Five-O* Producers, Harrington had already played a handful of bad guys on the series for years. From 1969-1971, he had parts in *Five-O* episodes "The Box," "The Late John Louisiana," "The Double Wall," "No Bottles...No Cans... No People," and "For a Million...Why Not?"[9] To Harrington, the role of Ben was "fun and interesting, because Ben was much more athletic than Kono or any of the other characters were. Ben was the one that did the running. He was very active physically, and that's what made him different from Kono and from Steve and from Danny." For Harrington, as an actor, it was fantastic, and Harrington considers himself very, very fortunate to have been brought in. When Harrington sat down with Lenny Freeman, the latter communicated to him that he envisioned Ben as a college graduate who had experience playing football and would be a member of the Five-O police force. Freeman asked to see Harrington after looking at footage of past roles he had played on the series. Leonard Freeman will always hold a special place in Harrington's heart:

"Freeman had a gift for sharing Hawaii, its culture, and its people with the world like no one else. He had a great love for Hawaii. He had a special love for us as a place, a good sensitivity to our diversity. And he brought that into play as far as the episodes were concerned. He was able to bring out the idiosyncratic meaning of Hawaii, the thing that made us different from other parts of the world – our great diversity, location in the Pacific, and central location of our geography. For me, having had some background in the historical process of Hawaii and the historical process of our nation, it was most gratifying to understand the creator of the show, Leonard Freeman himself, had a sensitivity to this and was able to bring it out in the episodes he created. It was that magic of diversity, the thing that makes Hawaii what it is, the Oriental process, the Western process, and the Pacific process. It all came together with drama that's significantly and consistently interesting and compelling. I am thankful to have had the opportunity to work with Lenny Freeman and those that have gone on, Jack, and, especially for me, James MacArthur. Jimmy was such a jewel of a person. Jack and the others have made such great, great, great contributions to Hawaii. They definitely have made us a better place and spread our history throughout the world."[10]

DID YOU KNOW • DID YOU KNOW • DID YOU KNOW • DID YOU KNOW • DID YOU

"Zulu" was a nickname from high school classmates.[11]

Zulu is regarded as the first Hawaiian to be a regular on a major TV series.

At about the same time that Zulu was honorary Chairperson for the American Cancer Society, Jack Lord was on its Board and asked Zulu to defer his involvement until a later date. Zulu refused.

Zulu made some nightclub appearances at Duke Kahanamoku's in Waikiki's International Marketplace while on Five-O *and enjoyed billing himself as "The One and Only Hawaiian Star of* Hawaii Five-O." *– a claim not well-received by Jack Lord.*

There was speculation that Zulu had some talks with Freeman about the possibility of his branching out in a new TV series of some kind apart from Hawaii Five-O. *It was never explored after Freeman's death in 1974.*

Zulu worked on occasion with Don Ho, was once a popular deejay in Honolulu, and took his nightclub act to the cruise-ship scene. He was heavily involved in most, if not all, aspects of putting his shows together.

Zulu's trait for creativity endeared him to Leonard Freeman.[12]

As a youngster, Harrington thought acting would be a fun thing to do.

Harrington was teaching Western Civilization and Hawaiian History at Punahou School in Honolulu when he was offered the part of Ben.

Harrington has the distinction of being the only living lead cast member of the original series and the only regular from the original series to appear in the reboot.[13]

A Glimpse into the Life of… Grace Park, One-on-One with An Actor Who Has Her Act Together

Hawaii Five-0's Grace Park (Kono) is an actress with a lot of grace (as her name suggests) as well as tremendous talent, and her entry into the world of acting is quite surprising. "I never wanted to be an actor," she told mytakeontv.com in 2012.[14] "When I was a kid, I think I wanted to be a research scientist. When I auditioned for the part of Kono, it was pilot season, and one of the projects was *Hawaii Five-0*. I ended up getting a screen test, so I had to fly to LA (from Vancouver) to screen test in front of all the executives, producers, and director, which was a mind numbingly, nerve-wracking experience. At the time, the Winter Olympics were happening in Vancouver, and I was watching these fantastic, exquisitely talented and trained figure skaters. They were competing live on the international stage, and they were just giving it their all every single time. And I thought, 'I have to go into a room with a handful of people and pretend to be a fake person. I can do that vs. me going out on a stage and performing for everyone internationally.' I also did a bit of research before my screen test."

And what a great screen test she gave, despite her fear. "People think acting is fast, fun, and glamorous. That's the fantasy that's created. The reality is you work 14-hour days for most of the year, take a quick break, then it's back to work. Also, people see us shooting at a mansion with a gorgeous view. You walk in, you're speechless. It's cool. But, that may happen only once a month. People also say, 'oh, I like Kono in a bikini' when, to be honest, I'm only in a bikini once or twice a year. Or, they say, 'she kicks butt.' And, I may actually only have one great scene. But part

Grace Park (photo credit: Hesham Foto –
http://www.heshamfoto.com, courtesy of
Tyman Stewart, Characters Talent Agency)

of that whole glamorous fantasy is the whole allure of Hawaii. The average person in Hawaii has the opposite experience from working on our show. We're not here for vacation; we're here to work." Park, without an acting background, got into the biz through modeling. "I'm pretty tall, so my mom convinced me to try this modeling school. I don't even think I knew what modeling was, so I was like 'ok.' I learned how to put on make-up, learned how to walk, very elementary stuff. I was not going to New York to model anytime for sure." From modeling school, she signed with a local Vancouver agency, which also had a small branch that produced commercials. "So, I went out and did some commercials. Since I was not an actor, commercials were not really acting to me. They were really an extension of modeling. I ended up booking a lot of commercials. So, the next step for them was, 'do you want to act? When I decided to go for it, I went fully into acting classes, scene study, improv, voice, Alexander technique… I didn't expect to be handed a job, and I knew I didn't know how to act. But I never wanted to be an actor. I didn't like delivering lines. I never did drama in high school. I'm just the opposite of that. What I did find was that I really liked being on set, because being on set was pretty different from being on a photo shoot. Photo shoots are a cool kind of visual. But I found that a set has a lot more people. They're not just shooting stills. An actor's shooting with living creatures, special effects, that kind of thing. There's a lot going on. All that type of stuff was fun. And I realized one day that, if I wanted to keep doing that, I'd have to learn how to deliver dialogue. So, I came in through the back stage door that leads to the alley. Whereas, I think most people want to come in the front door through the big lavish lobby. Also, I'm not like the typical actor. I'm more like, 'Can I be in the background? Can I be in the shadows? I just want to be here.' People think you act for the fame. I can't stand words like 'fame' or 'star' or 'celebrity.' Those are all like really bad words in my vocabulary."

As mentioned in Chapter 1, one major change to the character of Kono from the original *Five-O* was writing the part for a female, an idea Park supports. "I think there's certainly some diversity that comes from playing Kono as a female. And I think it's stronger for the show. Most of the roles for females when the original series aired were important, but they were not pivotal characters. It was a very different dynamic. There were a lot more males visible in television at that time, and the episodes were happening around them." But, things have changed, and Park has successfully brought originality to the role of Kono as a female, mostly due to her career in character-driven drama. She told mytakeontv.com:

"I like the challenge in a role. Sometimes, for me, though, it's much more fun to watch the episodes, especially when Kono is delivering exposition. It feels very different than other roles I've done. Kono really is her own character. When I did a show called *The Border* (Canadian drama), I played a homeland security agent liaison to the Canadian government. I feel like some of that attitude could come across, but Kono's a very different person. The role was very active, whereas, at times, the role of Kono has been pretty sedate. The character really has its own shape and its own presence. It's the challenge of doing a procedural, especially coming from my career of

Grace Park (photo credit: Hesham Foto – http://www. heshamfoto.com, courtesy of Tyman Stewart, Characters Talent Agency)

doing character-driven drama. It did look like a lot of character-driven drama in the pilot, with the background in terms of Steve McGarrett's family and the story of how the Five-0 task force came to be. But, in reality, in terms of this series, my character is number four. I really became aware of that when we shot 'Ha'awe Make Loa' (Death Wish, Season Three, Episode 9). Danny was removed from the rest of the crime to focus on the Victoria's Secret case. (It was sort of last minute, because the network wanted to tie in the Victoria's Secret show that was going to air the following night). Anyway, as I'm breaking down the scene, I'm feeling really weird, because I can't find the groove with this dialogue. I know something's different, but I can't figure it out. Then, it hit me. The dialogue used to be Danny's and, since he's not in the scene anymore, they put Kono in there. She's with McGarrett a lot in that episode. He talks to her differently. It's just those two together, and she's not the fourth person now. And I love that. I had to step up to the plate and change the way Kono was acting in order to make the scenes work."

As for stunts, Park has done her share of them. "I would say that doing the stunts was tricky in the beginning. You have to make it a safe world. You have to do a portion of stunts, and some people do more than others. Obviously actors like Tom Cruise and Jackie Chan do their own stunts. In one scene of the premiere for Season Three, Kono jumped onto a car and sprinted toward another car's windshield to shoot and kill a member of the Frank Delano (William Baldwin) team." Though a stunt girl completed the action, Park did stand on the pavement and jump onto the car. Could she have done it? Yes. "That one was easy, really simple I think. But, if I had done it and something had happened, if I had fallen and broken my leg, I'd be screwed for half the season. But we've done way more dangerous stunts than that." In Episode Seven, Season Three "Ohuna" (The Secret), there is a scene toward the end of the episode where Kono and bad guy Sean Winston (played by Carlo Rota) jump out of a moving vehicle. "That is a very dangerous stunt. People have died doing stunts like that. I have a stunt double that's so good. But stunt doubles are trained to do that. I'm trained to act. Even my stunt double was nervous doing that one, though. I look at it, then have to look away. If she had hit her head on the pavement... I couldn't put myself through that."

What she would love to do is help other people through her career. "I think it would be so rewarding to do a very good story about the Korean people, or any group of people, beyond violent circumstances and beyond the current political climate, to focus a bit more on humanity. I think something like that one of these days would be a good project, whether I'm acting in it or not. I kind of hope to be producing it instead. Now that would be something I would like to be a part of one day." Whether playing character-driven drama or not, Grace Park always has her act together.

OW • DID YOU KNOW • DID YOU KNOW • DID YOU KNOW • DID YOU KNOW • DID YO

Grace Park was quite popular as humanoid cylon Boomer/Athena in SyFy's Battlestar Galactica *(2004-2009).*

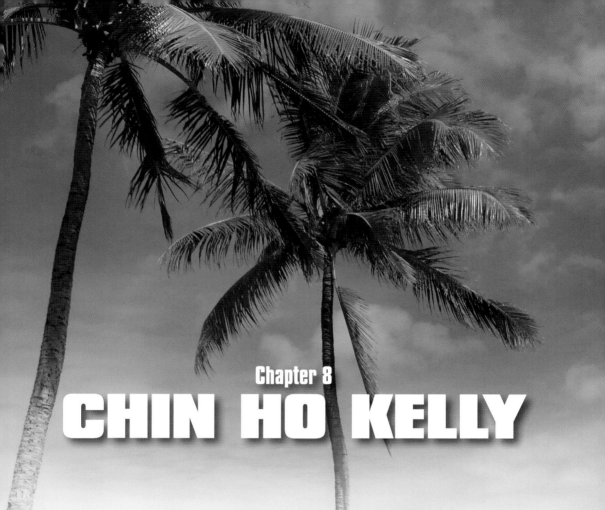

Chapter 8
CHIN HO KELLY

A Glimpse into the Life of... Kam Fong, A Man of Principle and High Integrity

There cannot be enough words to emphasize what kind of man Kam Fong was. If you can think of the highest honor to bestow upon someone, Fong would be the recipient of that award. There is an episode of the CBS TV series *Three Rivers* wherein a very obnoxious, arrogant patient constantly insults one of the doctors. And, there is a touching moment near the end of that episode where the patient, who is quite an intellectual, changes his attitude, makes an about-face, and pays the doctor the kindest, most noble compliment he is capable of giving another human being. He says, "You are a man of much substance and grace."[1] The author surmised that as an adequate description of the man Kam Fong.

Fong actually served as a police officer at the Honolulu Police Department (HPD) for 16 years before joining *Hawaii Five-O* as Chin Ho Kelly. Though this was not his first acting experience,[2] he embraced the role on the original series for ten seasons. The part seemed to fit him like a hand in a glove. The story goes that, when Leonard Freeman and the Director were

Above Left: Kam Fong Chun, who served as an HPD (Honolulu Police Department) officer from 1944-1959 (photo courtesy of HPD). Above Right: Officer Kam Fong Chun (left) and fellow police officer (photo courtesy of HPD)

casting, Fong walked in. Freeman simply looked up and said, "There's Chin Ho!" Freeman wanted him and got him.[3] James MacArthur told BBC Radio that Fong's real-life experiences as a police officer served him well in playing the role of Chin Ho and in putting what he had learned into practice in front of the cameras.[4] Fong was also a tremendous help for MacArthur in getting accustomed to living in Hawaii. MacArthur confided to the BBC, "Kam was a wonderful guy, a good friend, and he was also wonderful to me. I'd never been in the State of Hawaii before, except for one hour in my life, and he was especially wonderful at teaching those of us who were newcomers to the State about the old Hawaii that he knew before the War, and about the legends and things."[5] One thing Fong never spoke about was personal tragedies and heartaches. MacArthur also shared with BBC Radio that he had known Fong for quite a few years, and they were "special friends," but even he did not know about a heartbreak so close to Fong until the cast was shooting on location and Fong shared a very personal story with him. MacArthur revealed, "We were shooting at Diamond Head Cemetery. He said, 'Jimmy, come over here.' And he walked me over down the row of graves, and he pointed down, and I looked down. And he said, 'That's my wife and my children.' I had known him for six or seven years, and he had never mentioned anything. There we were, suddenly standing there, looking down at these graves, and I knew he had a (present) family and a wife, and so on. I was just speechless." What MacArthur did not know at the time was that Fong had lost his whole family, his first family, nearly 25 years before when, on June 8, 1944, two B-24 Liberators collided and crashed into his neighborhood,[6] killing twelve people, including his wife, Esther, and two small children (Marilyn, 4, and Donald, 2).[7]

Chapter 8 – CHIN HO KELLY

Dennis Chun (left) with Zulu at the Honolulu International Film Festival Awards Night, November 2003 (photo courtesy of Jerry Pickard)

DENNIS CHUN
ZOULOU
KAMANHI LIM
@ HIFF
AWARD
NIGHT
NOV '03

Fong was a sensitive, compassionate man, and his concern for others was immeasurable. He was a boilermaker at Pearl Harbor the day the Japanese bombed it, December 7, 1941, and helped in the rescue of sailors and personnel.[8] He had endured discrimination for being of Chinese heritage, perhaps by these same people, but he never thought of himself or how others may have hurt him.[9] Instead, he reported to work as usual following the attack and didn't leave for three days. He told the story this way, "I stood over the belly-up minelayer USS Ogalala, the only ship with a Hawaiian captain, and cried. I looked across the Bay and saw the Battleship USS Arizona burning, and I cried."[10] Fong was also a humble man. When the "Honolulu Advertiser" announced his death on October 30, 2002, a statement by his son Dennis Chun said, Fong "could never understand how 'a poor barefoot boy from Kalihi' could wind up on a Hollywood sound stage."[11] Toward the end of the original *Five-O* series, Fong became somewhat bored with his character and material, so he called it quits after ten years on the air.[12] The character, Chin Ho, was subsequently murdered in "A Death in the Family."[13] Chun's statement at the death of his father paid homage to how he died in real life. On behalf of his family, he spoke: "Like his character, our father faced his last battle with courage, determination, and a deep faith in God."[14] Sometime following his death, on May 18, 2013, perhaps way past time, Fong was elected into HPD's

Hall of Fame, nominated by HPD Major Raymond Ancheta.[15] It was an honor properly befitting such a worthy man. At the ceremony, son Dennis related how he had been asked in the past if it was difficult to fill his father's shoes as an actor. He simply responded, "That's the easy part. The hard part is trying to fill his shoes as a man."[16]

OW • DID YOU KNOW • DID YOU KNOW • DID YOU KNOW • DID YOU KNOW • DID YO

Kam Fong was a native Hawaiian.[17]

Fong was taught incorrectly how to spell his real name, Kam Tong Chun ("golden temple" in Chinese), so he changed his name to Kam Fong Chun.[18]

When Hawaii Five-O filmed in Hong Kong or Singapore, the locals spoke to Fong in Chinese, but he couldn't speak a word of the Chinese language.[19]

A Glimpse into the Life of... Daniel Dae Kim, an Actor's Actor

Korean-American actor Daniel Dae Kim (born in South Korea)[20] grew up in a bilingual household, speaking Korean at home and English in school.[21] He is proud of his Korean heritage and pays homage to it with the East West Players, a stage company that the "New York Times" once called "the nation's pre-eminent Asian American theater troupe." Kim's first project with the Players was in 2002 in *The Tempest.*[22] Discovering acting while at Bryn Mawr College in Pennsylvania, Kim went on to earn his Master's Degree from New York University's Tisch School of the Arts. He also studied at the National Theater Institute at the Eugene Theater Center before graduating from Tisch with a Master's Degree in Acting. His first big stage role was with a Pan Asian Repertory Theatre as Torvald in *A Doll's House.*[23] His background in stage all over the world is testament to the fact that he takes acting very seriously. Not many television actors can boast the projects Kim has been a part of in the theatre. These works include *Romeo and Juliet, The School for Wives* (with the National Asian American Theatre Company), *The Chang Fragments, Golden Child* (in 2000 with the East West Players), and *A Midsummer Night's Dream,* to name a few.[24] In 2001, he even directed *Hamlet*, saying "I like directing for the stage. It's something that I started to do in New York and would like to explore further when I get the chance. I also write regularly, but it's mainly in the form of a journal I like to keep.[25] Kim told famright.com, "There's something about being in a house with an audience and having immediate feedback. I started acting because of that energy. It's what feeds me on stage and informs my choices. What's great in theatre is that you can sustain the arc of a character for a full three

Daniel Dae Kim (photo credit: Meryl Hollar, from the author's personal collection)

hours, whereas in film or TV, you have to create that arc in little pieces, usually out of sequence."[26] In 2011, he told Christie Wilson of the "Honolulu Pulse," "Quite literally, I spent eight years in New York after college doing theater, most of it off and off-off Broadway and often for nothing. I'm very in touch with what it means to be a theater artist."[27] And his stage work has been impressive, including appearing in Chekhov's *Ivanov*.[28] In 2009, during a hiatus from *Lost,* he appeared at the Royal Albert Hall in *The King and I*.[29] With acting being his passion, the author asked him in 2013 about his then last play. A project he produced in Hawaii, it was called *Hold These Truths,* and it was, in Kim's own words, "a one-man show based on the life of Gordon Hirabayashi, who was a conscientious objector to World War II. Hirabayashi refused to go into the internment camps when the Japanese Americans were ordered to do so. And he was, in my opinion, a hero. I was able to spring Joel de la Fuente from New York to star, and I was happy to do that."[30]

Kim's first feature film project was *American Shaolin: King of the Kickboxers II* (1993), while his first television appearance was in 1994, with a guest spot on *Law and Order*.[31] After *Lost's* successful six seasons, Kim remained on the Islands and was offered the role of Chin Ho Kelly. While playing the Chin Ho role, in 2012, Kim visited Korea as a Cultural Ambassador for the US Pavilion at the Yeosu Expo. Hancinema.net reported that, during the event, Kim commented that when he started acting, "most writers did not have Asian actors in mind when they penned scripts, so it was tough to pass auditions. When they were looking to fill Asian parts, it was still grueling, because I had to compete with a multitude of Asian and Asian-American actors."[32] Known for his accessibility, Kim stated during the Sunset on the Beach premiere for Season Three of the reboot *Five-0* that people have gotten used to his being on the Island and don't pay much attention to him. Also known for his community involvement, in 2011, he made an appearance at the Actors and Artists Fund Launch Party for the Honolulu Theatre for Youth (HTY). Funds raised for the program are used to pay "a living wage" to the actors, directors, playwrights, composers, and designers of HTY. Kim told the "Honolulu Pulse" at the time, "It's because I call it home. I care about my home and this is the only professional theater in Hawaii, and it's worth supporting. It's good not only for the community but for the theater artists to have a place where they can come and act."[33] Of the reboot *Five-0* he has said, "One of the nice things about our version is that it respects and pays homage to the original but also makes changes to kind of accommodate today's sensibilities."[34]

As for awards, this talented actor shared a 2006 Screen Actors Guild Award for Best Ensemble for *Lost*. While on *Lost*, he also was presented with Outstanding Performance by an Actor awards by the Korean American Coalition, including an AZN Asian Excellence Award, a Multicultural Prism Award, and a Vanguard Award. In 2009, he won the KoreAm Journal Achievement Award in Arts and Entertainment.[35]

Currently, Kim's production company 3AD is developing a feature film project on the adaptation of *Escaping North Korea: Defiance and Hope in the World's Most Repressive Country* by Mike Kim. The work chronicles Mike Kim's work in leading refugees to safety through a modern day Underground Railroad.[36]

Truly Daniel Dae Kim is an actor's actor.

OW • **DID YOU KNOW** • **DID YOU KNOW** • **DID YOU KNOW** • **DID YOU KNOW** • **DID YO**

Daniel Dae Kim studied Korean while playing the role of Jin-Soo Kwok in Lost *and, by the fifth season, mastered the language he hadn't spoken since he was a child.*[37]

Occasionally, Daniel Dae Kim helps HTY with acting workshops.[38]

Besides his work with the HTY, Daniel Dae Kim is quite active with the National Asian American Theatre Company.[39]

When the Special Olympics was held in Pyeongchang, Korea in 2013, Daniel Dae Kim served as Promotional Ambassador.[40]

Daniel Dae Kim once co-owned The Counter Honolulu in Kahala Mall.[41]

In October, 2014, Daniel Dae Kim launched a CBS Studios-based production company called 3AD, which gives him a two-year first-look deal in developing projects for cable and network television.[42]

Chapter 9
DANNO

A Glimpse into the Life of... James MacArthur, An Actor of Generous Passion

James MacArthur (James Gordon MacArthur – "Jimmy") played Danny (Danno) Williams in the original *Hawaii Five-O*, and he was an inspiration to many, many people. One of those people was Al Harrington. Harrington, who made the successful transition from teaching Western Civilization/Hawaiian History to acting, credited MacArthur as being "very helpful to me in working scenes and delivering lines to make them more realistic. The whole acting experience was aided by his acting experiences and his willingness to help. He didn't force that help, but when we needed it, he would come in and give us some suggestions from his vast experiences." Margaret Doversola agreed, "The original Danny, Jimmy MacArthur, was such a sweet, nice, down-to-earth guy. There was no attitude, no ego, just a really great guy. I hated to go to his funeral. It was so sad to see them all dying."[2]

MacArthur left *Hawaii Five-0* a year before its final season, stating, "The stories became more bland and predictable and presented less and less challenge to me as an actor."[3] MacArthur began his career in 1955 with "Deal a Blow," an episode of the TV series *Climax!* But it was his work of only two to three days in Leonard Freeman's low-budget Western film *Hang 'Em High* that led to his casting in the iconic role of Danny Williams. [4]

As the reboot *Five-0* held its first Sunset on the Beach premiere,

James MacArthur (photo courtesy of Carol Miller Keale, from her personal collection)

MacArthur shared the following message through his beloved friend Harrington:

"Good evening, everyone! I hope you're all enjoying a fine Hawaiian sunset, and I'm sorry I can't be there with you tonight.

"Ever since I saw the script for the pilot, I've been very excited about this new *Hawaii Five-0*. From that first moment, I knew CBS had another winner on its hands.

"I can remember back to when Lenny Freeman called to invite me to participate in the original version. My first thought was, 'Great! If I'm lucky, this is my free ticket to 13 weeks in Hawaii. Count me in!'

"Little did I know that 40 years later, people would still be calling out to me to 'Book 'em, Danno!' wherever I go, and that *Hawaii Five-0* would become a worldwide phenomenon, an indelible part of our modern culture, ready tonight to launch a bold new incarnation.

"I think I can confidently speak for Lenny, Jack, Kam, Zulu, and the rest of the original gang, as well as myself, in saying that we're all just delighted with the outstanding caliber and sheer talent of the people involved with the new *Five-0*. It's very heartening to see our legacy now in the hands of the terrific people you see before you tonight.

"I'm looking forward to making an appearance in the new show when the time is right, and I can't wait to see what the writers have in store for me. In the meantime, I'll be watching each week, eagerly anticipating the further

Chapter 9 – DANNO

adventures of the new *Five-0* team.

"May you all enjoy Hawaii and its fabulous people as much as I continue to do to this day, and may your association with *Hawaii Five-0* be as successful and fulfilling for you as mine has been for me!

"And remember: 'Be there! Aloha!'"

"Be there! Aloha" was the

A candid shot of (left to right) Kam Fong, Moe Keale, and James MacArthur (photo courtesy of Carol Miller Keale, from her personal collection)

phrase Jack Lord used at the end of each episode as previews aired.

Karen Rhodes, author of *Booking Hawaii Five-O*, shared her experiences with MacArthur, "We mainly discussed books via email. He apparently enjoyed reading about the Civil War. As an actor, he was a very practical sort, i.e., 'just do the job.' He wasn't into 'Method' acting or any of that. I think Jack Lord was more the 'Method' type. At the *Five-O* Burbank convention in 1996, I asked Jim if he had any way of particularly preparing himself for the role of Dan Williams. His very practical – and a bit acerbic – reply was, 'Just say the *(bleep)* lines!' Question answered, sure enough. I get the idea that he thought 'Method' was for the birds. The best insight, and what I remember best about him, was that he had a great sense of humor and mischief. The first day of the Burbank half of the *Five-O* Convention, the Convention Chair and Organizer delegated to me the task of finding Jim and giving him his plane ticket to Honolulu for the second half of the Convention. When I approached him, he was a bit skeptical (as all actors have to be, with the fans that follow and sometimes stalk them). I simply said that the Convention Chair had asked me to deliver his plane ticket, and with that, he warmed right up. Later, the Convention Chair and I were walking with him in the lobby, and the Convention Chair was getting rather gushy about Dan Williams, apparently her favorite character. She was talking about how sensitive the character was and yadda yadda, and I could see Jim rolling his eyes. So I added, '. . . and sarcastic,' because Dan Williams *was* sarcastic, and that was the characteristic about him that I liked best! Jim nearly stumbled and fell as he burst out laughing when I said that. I think that's one thing that induced him to befriend me - that, and the fact that everyone knew that my brother had just died a couple weeks before, and I was still fragile from that, a bad experience for the entire family. But Jim was sympathetic. I'll always remember that."[5]

What a treasure – James MacArthur, a friend to all.

On November 6, 2003, James MacArthur was honored by the Hawaii International Film Festival with the Film in Hawaii Award for his significant contributions to the local film industry.

MacArthur passed away before he could make an appearance on the Five-0 *reboot.*[6]

A Glimpse in the Life of... Scott Caan, Variety Is the Spice of Life

You never know where you're going to see Scott Caan next. Caan came to *Five-0,* much like MacArthur, from a background of stage, film, and television. Most notably, his roles have included parts in HBO's *Entourage* and the Warner Brothers' George Clooney/Matt Damon/Brad Pitt *Ocean's Eleven, Ocean's Twelve,* and *Ocean's Thirteen* films.[7]

According to the *Hawaii Five-0* DVD, Season One, behind-the-scenes, Caan never actually read with O'Loughlin for the part of Williams. The two apparently just clicked when they met following Caan's taking of the role. Caan has been known to use his hiatus time away from the show in performance of perhaps his most passionate role – that of playwright. Indeed, while on hiatus prior to Season Three, Caan spent at least a portion of his summer break performing at the Falcon Theatre in Burbank, California, in a play he wrote himself entitled *No Way Around But Through*. Caan described the project to Patricia Foster Rye of the "LA Stage Times," "This play is about serious, serious issues, about people who are messed up since their childhoods. It's about a very strange relationship between a mother and a son and even stranger relationships with other characters. The idea is that we're all in trouble for a reason, and the big question is, 'how did we end up the way we are?'"[8] The play centers on Caan's character, Jacob, who discovers his girlfriend (played by Robyn Cohen from *The Life Aquatic*) is pregnant. Jacob blames his mother (played by Melanie Griffith) for his inability to commit to

Scott Caan (right) greets Alex O'Loughlin and Grace Park at the very first scene and blessing ceremony for Hawaii Five-0 (photo courtesy of George F. Lee, "Honolulu Star-Advertiser")

his girlfriend. Ultimately, both Jacob and his girlfriend end up at his mother's place, trying to find out why he is as he is. Griffith had nothing but praise for Caan in an interview with "The LA Times," saying, "I love the way it's (the play) written. I like the way Scott writes. I think he's really gifted."[9] The play also starred Val Lauren[10] and Bre Blair[11]. And, it's published by the Dramatists Play Service. (Caan's 2010 romantic play *Two Wrongs* was also published in 2012 by the same company).[12] Caan revealed to Rye, "To have a play published and know someone might produce your play in the future, to me that's kind of the ultimate thing. And when I kept submitting my plays, and they wouldn't get published for whatever reason—too small a theater or not enough reviews or not enough people came and saw it or the right person at the publishers hadn't read it yet—in a sense it made me go, 'Why am I doing this?' Now that my plays are with Dramatists Play Service, I want to keep writing plays as much as possible and also go back and have some of my earlier works published."[13]

Caan has also written indie film projects. *Mercy*, starring Dylan McDermott (*The Practice)* and Wendy Glenn, is a romantic project that also stars Caan's father, actor James Caan (*The Godfather).*[14] The younger Caan is also Producer of the film. Other indie projects written by Caan include a comedy involving the Playboy Mansion called *Chasing the Party*, a boxing project called *The Fight,* and a drama entitled *Least Common Demoninator.*[15] Caan has also shown promise as a Director. Thus far in his career, he has directed indie projects *Dallas 362*[16] and *The Dog Problem* (both of which he wrote). *Dallas 362* is a film about friendship which also stars Jeff Goldblum and Val Lauren. *The Dog Problem* is a comedy about a writer who gets a terrier to help him with his depression. (Caan plays the writer's friend).[17] In the summer of 2013, Caan co-starred in Rubbertree Productions' *3 Geezers!* The project is about an actor who checks into The Coconuts convalescent home while researching an upcoming role. When he becomes the object of numerous resident pranks, he "gets even" with the help of some friends.[18] The project was released to DVD on August 13, 2013.

Another perhaps little-known fact about Caan is that he is actively involved with two surfing charities. One is Surfer's Healing, which therapeutically uses surfing to help children diagnosed with autism. The charity was founded by Israel and Danielle Paskowitz after their three year-old son, Isaiah, was diagnosed with autism. Israel, a former surfer, stumbled upon this unique approach by accident while surfing with Danielle and Isaiah. He decided to start the Surfer's Healing Foundation as a way to help other children cope with autism.[19] The other Foundation Caan works with is Life Rolls On,[20] which helps surfers with spinal cord injuries to surf again. Jesse Billauer is the organization's Founder. Of his work with these charities, Caan told "Los Angeles Confidential," "At the end of the day, I'm more grateful to be a part of these than just about anything I have. It's hard to talk about them and not be completely humbled. If you know how to surf or you can swim, and you get a kick out of helping people, then I can't imagine a better day."[21]

KNOW • DID YOU KNOW • DID YOU KNOW • DID YOU KNOW • DID YOU KNOW • DID YO

Caan was trained at the Playhouse West School and Repertory Theatre, as was Val Lauren.

In the Fall of 2001, Caan starred in a play at Playhouse West that he wrote, co-directed, and starred in called Almost Love.

Caan would someday like to own his own theatre.[22]

In 2011, Caan was nominated for a Golden Globe Award for Hawaii Five-0 for Best Performance by an Actor in a Supporting Role in a Series, Mini-Series, or Motion Picture Made for Television.

Actor Michael Shanks (Saving Hope, Smallville, Stargate Universe, Stargate Atlantis, Stargate SG-1) auditioned for the role of Danny Williams.[23]

Melanie Griffith plays the role of Danny Williams' mother in the reboot series.[24]

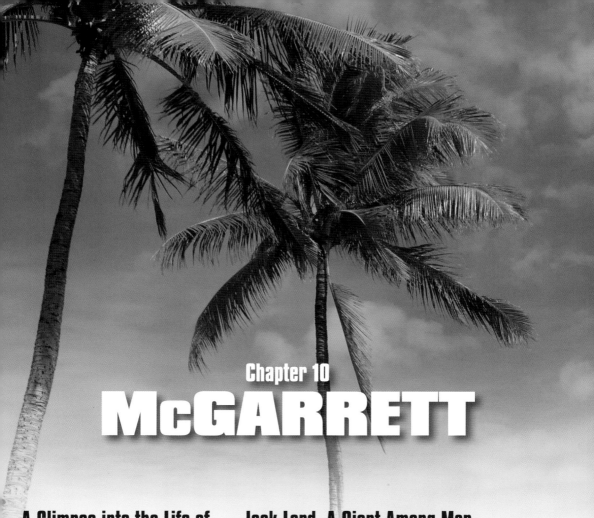

Chapter 10
McGARRETT

A Glimpse into the Life of... Jack Lord, A Giant Among Men

Jack Lord a. k. a. Steve McGarrett was not an easy man to know. He and his wife, Marie, quietly lived in the Kahala area of Oahu in the years after *Five-O*. Helping them was Margaret Doversola. Doversola continued her role as Lord's Assistant until his death in 1998, after which she continued to spend time with Marie by taking her to lunch once a week. In a phone conversation with the author, Doversola confided, "I knew Jack Lord as a boss and got on with him very well. He didn't always get on with a lot of people, so I was happy at the end that I could work for him and do what he needed. Jack was spot. He was tough. The fact that they teased his hair was weird. But he cared about how he looked and what he did. He *was* what you hear. He was a perfectionist. He was very hard to get on with if you didn't do your job right. But if you did your job right, he was fine. He was pretty self-deprecating, except when he wanted his own way."[1]

Doversola confessed that one never told Lord he couldn't get what he wanted. He always had to be given alternatives, and "no" was not an option. Working for Lord involved a lot of hard work, a lot of overtime, a lot of stress, and extra hours (often working 'til midnight) without getting paid. But Doversola loved it. "Whatever Jack Lord did, he did it really well, and when Leonard Freeman died, Jack became the boss. When he became the boss, things got done just the way he wanted. And that's how he liked it. He knew what he wanted. And he always said, 'Hawaii's the star. The crime is the story. And I don't want to hear anything personal about McGarrett in the show.' There was a lot of Hawaiiana,[2] a lot of good feelings, a lot of camaraderie, a lot of help on the set. Jack always knew what script changes there were, because he instigated them. He also knew I did those changes all on my own. And, when I was really, really, really in trouble, and we were doing script changes really fast, Jack would send someone from the stage where they were working to my office to help put the changes together. He was into everything. He definitely knew what was going on. Sure, there were some run-ins, even with Freeman. There were times when Jack wanted to walk, or Freeman wanted him to walk. But they stuck together. And, it worked out really well. From time to time, Jack would also have disagreements with some of the actors. He would call them into the office and give them hell. And then he'd come to the door and wink and say, 'Hey, Margaret, you got any coffee?' And I'd make him coffee, and he'd come out and wink again and take the coffee. He was very tough and very strong. There were people who hated his guts. But when

Right: Jack Lord and Moe Keale in a candid moment between takes (photo courtesy of Carol Miller Keale, from her personal collection). Inset: Jack Lord advertisement from the rodeo circuit, 1964 (anonymous fan contribution) Below: Jack Lord painting "Aloha Ke Akua" (photo courtesy of Hawaii Gallery of Fine Art)

you got down to working with him one on one, he was very fair. Jack loved Hawaii and its people, and everything on the show was local. The focus was on "Hawaiian" crime,[3] and the stories were Hawaiiana stories. Jack held the reins. He did it the way he thought. And it was successful for a lot of different reasons - I think basically because he cared about Hawaii." Lord even wrote about the love he had for the State in a 1977 article for ASTA Holiday (the American Society of Travel Agents). In it, he said, 'It's (Hawaii) as close to Paradise as you can find in this world. I'm very grateful to have finally settled on this as the

place where we're going to spend the rest of our lives. Living in Hawaii was decided for us, my wife Marie and me, by God, and by CBS. I have always believed in the metaphysical premise that 'the place you seek is seeking you – the place you need needs you.'"[4] John Fischer at gohawaii.about.com quoted Lord from that ASTA article, "People say to me all the time, 'Do you like Hawaii?' and I say, 'No, I love Hawaii.' I find the people here very friendly. There's a sweetness, a gentleness, a naivete that is found nowhere else. It's a marvelous mixture of Polynesian and Caucasian and Oriental, a strange and interesting blend of unique people. I think 'Golden People' suits them perfectly. Gold doesn't tarnish."[5] Lord had more to write, "We love the place – the fresh, clean air. We love the sparkling blue sea forty feet from our lanai – the birds and flowers (there are over three hundred varieties of flowering plants and trees). We love the people and their Polynesian and Oriental backgrounds, customs, old ways. We love Oahu, where we live, and the neighboring Islands for their special charms. Who can walk around the waterfront of Lahaina on Maui and not be caught up in the history of this ancient whaling port with its jail, quaint streets, and Pioneer Inn? Nor can one remain unimpressed with God and nature after standing on the lip of the Halemaumau Crater on the Big Island and watching the fireworks. And the place we love most – in Hawaii, or anywhere else – is our home."[6] That was truly a touching sentiment and a great tribute. Lord's love for the Islands is shown by the legacy he left behind - $40 million to the Hawaii Community Foundation to benefit designated charities and nonprofit organizations, a gift whose benefits continue through this day. These charities and nonprofit organizations include Hospice Hawaii (which receives several hundred thousand dollars a year), PBS Hawaii (receives nearly $30,000 annually), the Hawaii Lions Eye Foundation (on the verge of shutting its doors before the arrival of its gift), ARC in Hawaii (for people with developmental disabilities), the Bishop Museum (for studying and preserving the history of Hawaii), the Hawaiian Humane Society, Honolulu Academy of the Arts, Salvation Army Hawaii, St. Francis Hospice Care Center, and the United Service Organizations (supporting the troops). [7] Lord may have had a big heart for giving, but the Hawaiian people (and others) also had a big heart for him. Kahala Mall donated a space of land for the erection of a bust in memory of Jack Lord. After Lord died, there were two *Hawaii Five-O* conventions, where money was raised to erect the statue. Actor Doug Mossman (who appeared in both original and reboot episodes of the series)[8] and Lynn Liverton, a fan from England, helped greatly in seeing this project through to completion. According to Doversola, Liverton raised money from her own country, and she was the one responsible for getting the bust made.

One very unique quality about Jack Lord was that he worked with "regular" people to turn them into actors. They were hired at Lord's word, without an acting resume of any kind. Doversola shared, "He loved to get these actors on the show that he really respected and he really liked. [9] He was a different kettle of fish and had his own way of doing things." He met these people everywhere. He met Kinau Wilder[10] at a party. He liked what he saw and brought her to the set. He showed her what it was all about, got her on stage with a part, and literally taught her how to be an actor. You don't see stars of TV shows doing that these days." Around 1973, Native Hawaiian Jimmy Borges was singing his unique music[11] at Keone's when Lord came to see him about being on the show. Borges shared his story in a recent interview, "He came backstage and told me he liked my music. He said, 'You know, I really like the way you handle your language. You seem to make up the lyrics on the spot.' He said, 'That would be very helpful to us if you become an actor. Would you like to give it a try?' I said, 'I'm not that crazy about acting.' He said, 'You can create your dialogue right there on the spot and feed it to the next actor.' He said, 'It would save us a lot of time in writing dialogue.'"[12] Borges gave it a try, and he liked it. " I enjoyed it, once I got into it, because whatever I wanted the characters I played to be, that's what they were. The Directors were really good about that.

They allowed me to create the characters. It was really fun. The characters I played were usually bad guys. You have much better dialogue with those parts anyway. The good guys don't have a lot to say. Besides, Jack was always the good guy with all the good lines. And, that's the way it should be." Borges went on to guest star in 15 episodes of the series. His favorite character was Kum Chi, the head of the local Syndicate. Borges wore a three-piece suit and wore phony, ornate jewelry for the role.[13] He confided, "After my first couple of shows, they would send me a script with a few suggestions. We'd always come to a common conclusion. When we filmed the show, I would sing from 10pm til 4am. Then, when I got through, I would go home, take a quick shower, and go to the set. I would try to catch up on my sleep in between set-ups."

Another actor Lord trained was Moe Keale. "Keale was a big, burly Hawaiian guy, and he was pure Hawaiian. He was an electrician on the set, and Jack tried to convince him that he should be an actor. But, he was always up ladders, working. This one time, Jack got Moe down off the ladder and gave him some lines. Jack really liked him." So, he taught him how to be an actor. In an email from her home in Hawaii, Carol Miller Keale, Moe's widow, shared that Moe guest-starred on the series for ten years in various roles before he took the regular role of Truck Kealoha in the final year of the series. She confided, "Jack Lord and his wife loved my husband and took us out to dinner quite a few times. We were very fortunate to be friends with Jack and Marie."[14] When Moe and Carol were married, Jack Lord gave them a lithograph he had painted entitled "The Loner." He signed the front of the lithograph and wrote on the back, "For Carol and Moe – May all your dreams come true – Aloha Ke Akua, Jack Lord, December 14, 1980."[15] He also signed the front, which included a quote from Henry David Thoreau: "If a man does not keep pace with his companions, perhaps it is because he hears a different drummer. Let him step to the music he hears, however measured or far away." A little-known fact about Lord was that his first love was painting. It remained so throughout his life, and he was quite a gifted artist. Some of his paintings were acquired by the Metropolitan Museum of Art and by the British Museum.[16]

Lord sometimes experienced some ego issues. Doversola shared one such story that involved actor William Smith, who played recurring character Detective James "Kimo" Carew on the show. When new actors came to their roles, Lord wanted the script rewritten so that they would have more dialogue. But, when they got too much, Lord took action. He had Doversola bring her typewriter to the set so that he could rewrite some of the dialogue. In the end,

Doversola had the arduous task of going to the actors' trailers the next day to inform them that everything had changed. All the dialogue they spent so much time learning had overnight become one-liners. Lord kept all the good dialogue for himself. Another story about Lord and dialogue involved actor Rod Aiu. Aiu shared with the author that Lord used cue cards with his lines on them, and whenever Aiu would make a guest appearance, Lord would usually try to trick him or trip him up in some way so that he would stumble over or forget his lines altogether. Lord tested him. But, Aiu always got his lines right, which highly impressed Lord.[17] Yet another story involved Location Manager Randy Spangler, who once took Lord out on a hobie cat. Spangler shared via email, "We were shooting the opening to the show, and the stunt guys couldn't get the balance right for lifting the hull. We kept crashing. So, Jack said, 'Let's give it a try.' The first take was perfect. I lifted Jack up on the one-hull maneuver. He was a natural. When we came to the dock, he got off and went to fight crime. Cut…one take…perfectly done…fun day!"[18]

Another little known fact about Lord was that, in a way, he started the first *Hawaii Five-0* Sunset on the Beach. According to Doversola, he was very good at dealing with the press. Prior to each season, there would be a dinner or drinks of some sort for the press, where Lord would give them some idea of what to expect in the upcoming season. These events were held all over Oahu, from hotels to the studio to a set location. "We would spend hours in the office preparing little toys and little paperwork, little things he gave away. One year, we gave a bobby whistle, the long thin one, and we stuck '*Hawaii Five-O*' on all these whistles. Another time, we had this little red Old English scroll written in Chinese (because Wo Fat was a spy for the Red Chinese). I think it was the name of the show and the season number. And, of course, we showed the press the first episode of the season. "Jack was really good. He did a lot of good PR." He also attended a lot of charity events and parties, especially for the military. "He was a Merchant Marine in his day and was big on the military. And, if he ever needed something from the military, they always gave it to him (without having to go through the Department of Defense)."

Lord also wasn't shy when it came time to doing stunts. Doversola shared that, for one scene in the pilot, Lord was underwater, totally deprived of all hearing and sight, for quite a period of time (though he did have something in his mouth so that he could get air). She summed up her experiences with *Five-O* simply by saying, "It was a lot of fun. We had a good time."[19]

Jack Lord's real name was John Joseph Patrick Ryan.

Jack Lord got into acting by filming maritime training films. His first acting job was on Broadway.

Jack Lord auditioned for the role of Captain James T. Kirk in the Star Trek *television series before landing the role of Steve McGarrett.*

Jack Lord studied at the Actors Studio.[20]

According to Jack Lord, another star was originally signed to play McGarrett, but CBS couldn't sell the package. Then, the network came to him and offered him the part, paying the other star off. After Jack Lord was signed to play McGarrett, CBS took the pilot to New York, and it sold out in only a few hours.[21]

According to Carol Miller Keale, if actors didn't know their lines on set, Jack Lord would yell at them in front of everyone else. "Marie helped Jack learn his lines every night for the next day. She woke him early in the morning with a small breakfast. He would go for a short walk, then come back to their condo and eat a bigger, healthy breakfast that would give his day a really good start."[22]

The April 8, 1980 edition of "Daily Variety" featured a full-page ad by Jack Lord, thanking the network and everyone involved for Hawaii Five-O's" *12-year run on the air. The headline for the ad read, "Mahalo Nui Loa" (Thank You Very Much).*

In 1980, after Hawaii Five-O, *Jack produced and directed* M-Station Hawaii. *According to an email from Carol Miller Keale, "It was filmed off Makai Pier near Sea Life Park. The basic idea was there was a group of oceanographers that worked off the pier, but they were undercover police officers. Moe was the only carry-over from Five-O. His role was the first part that called for an educated Hawaiian (Moe had two college degrees). Jack even had a mini-submarine made for the pilot that actually functioned. All the actors had really ugly custom-made wet suits that were orange with yellow stripes. Then, we found out that sharks will attack an orange wet suit and ignore a black one. It became the joke of the show. Unfortunately, the pilot was not purchased for a series. Jack found that very upsetting."[23]*

A Glimpse into the Life of... Alex O'Loughlin, An Actor with a Purpose

Australian actor Alex O'Loughlin (original spelling O'Lachlan)[24] came to play Lieutenant Commander Steve McGarrett through a myriad of roles that show off his diversity in talent and depth of character exploration. A graduate of the prestigious National Institute of Dramatic Art (NIDA) in Kensington, Australia, O'Loughlin was nominated by the Australian Film Institute in 2005 for Best Lead Actor in Television for the Australian mini-series *The Incredible Journey of Mary Bryant* and for a Logie Award for Most Outstanding Actor in a Drama Series in 2006 for the same project.[25] The acting bug bit at an early age. In 2010, O'Loughlin told "Vanity Fair Italia's" Fransesca Scorcucchi, "As a kid, I used to go to theatre with my mom. Once I saw *Joseph and the Amazing Technicolor Dreamcoat*, and I remember thinking, 'this is what I want to do when I grow up.'"[26] In primary school, when he reportedly appeared in a play and sang "Simply Irresistible," he was hooked by the laughter and applause of the audience,[27] telling Scorcucchi, "The most

Left: Alex O'Loughlin (right) with Olympic Snowboarding Bronze Medalist Chris Klug (left) and musician Alex Band (center) at Donate Life Awards arrivals, 2010 (photo credit: Twin Triumph Productions, LLC). Right: Alex O'Loughlin accepts his Person of the Year Award from Donate Life, 2010 (photo credit: Twin Triumph Productions, LLC)

Left: Alex O'Loughlin shares a joke with the audience at the Paley Center, Donate Life Awards, 2010 (photo credit: Twin Triumph Productions, LLC). Right: Alex O'Loughlin speaks from the podium at the Paley Center, Donate Life Awards, 2010 (photo credit: Twin Triumph Productions, LLC)

beautiful thing was to 'feel' the public, even if I couldn't see it, because of the lights on the stage."[28] Even so, O'Loughlin did not immediately pursue a career in acting, choosing rather to work at odd jobs, including that of a bartender, a plumber's apprentice, a waiter, and a builder.[29] He told "The Canberra Times" in 2005 that he didn't immediately pursue a theatrical career because he didn't think he was good enough.[30] However, he began to take his dream a bit more seriously when, while pretending to "narrate" a rugby match, a friend reminded him he truly was an actor and needed to do something about it.[31]

O'Loughlin's first real acting job came after graduating from NIDA and making a guest appearance in Australia's Channel Ten crime drama *White Collar Blue*.[32] A breakout project for the young actor was the starring role in *The Oyster Farmer* (where he met and worked with legendary Australian actor Jack Thompson). The award-nominated performance in *The Incredible Journey of Mary Bryant* soon followed. Another early project was *Man-Thing*. It was important to his career in that he again worked with Jack Thompson, along with Jack's son Patrick, and American film Director Brett Leonard. Together, these four formed Honour Bright Productions and set out to produce its maiden, and thus far, only project, *Feed*. The younger Thompson told "The Australian," "'Honour Bright' is how we feel about each other. It's a very old Australian phrase that we feel is representative of us as a group of friends. We feel we have honour bright."[33] And, according to "The Australian," the idea for the project came from O'Loughlin and the younger Thompson after they watched the documentary *Fat Girls and Feeders*.[34] A move to America was inevitable – but not easy. As O'Loughlin revealed to connectv.com in 2009, "There was

Left: Alex O'Loughlin in a playful pose for the press at the Paley Center, Donate Life Awards, 2010 (photo credit: Twin Triumph Productions, LLC). Right: Alex O'Loughlin works the red carpet (from the author's personal collection)

a point when I was living on my mate Sam Gould's couch for over a year… I'd run out of money. A Ducati motorcycle, the only thing I owned, had been stolen and the insurance money had run out. I couldn't get arrested in this town (Los Angeles)."[35] What kept him going was something he remembered his grandfather told him, "Put your head down, and keep working, son, and you'll get what's coming to you."[36] And push through he did. In 2007, O'Loughlin was cast in the role of Kevin Hiatt in FX's *The Shield.* This solid performance was followed by a leading man role as vampire detective Mick St. John in the cult favorite *Moonlight.* Following that series' untimely demise, O'Loughlin appeared in an episode of *Criminal Minds* as serial killer Vincent Rowlings. He told mytakeontv.com at the time that Executive Producer/Showrunner Simon Mirren wrote the character with him in mind and asked him if he'd be willing to read for the role and take it.[37] He said in the 2009 interview with Amrie Cunningham, "I was really captured in what Simon wrote. I was really captured in Vincent, this character's pursuit of salvation, because he seems like such an unredeemable character – like the acts that he perpetrates are unforgiveable, and perhaps they are. I think the spirit of the man himself is beyond salvation and that's what I as the actor went for."[38]

The Shield and *Criminal Minds* boast some of O'Loughlin's best work. But, the very best, and most rewarding work for O'Loughlin (also the author's favorite role) was yet to come. In 2009, Executive Producer/Showrunner Carol Barbee cast O'Loughlin as the star of her new series *Three Rivers* in the leading man role of Dr. Andy Yablonski, heart transplant surgeon. The role was far different from anything O'Loughlin had tackled to date. It was based on real-life heart transplant surgeon Dr. Gonzo Gonzales-Stawinski, and it gave O'Loughlin a platform to speak out for a good cause. At the time, he said, "I think this is an important platform, this is an important cause, and being in this role has given me an opportunity to share a message about organ donation."[39] In a 2009 MySpace entry, O'Loughlin wrote, "I have the chance to give the gift of life, which I believe is the greatest gift of all."[40] He also shared with connectv. com, "I realized [through this show] that physicians have the capacity to love the unloveable. The most awful person you can imagine could be lying in the hospital bed, and the physician will say to them, 'everything will be OK.'"[41] In December of that year, his MySpace entry was, "I realized immediately how important this story was and would be. This, the story of so many different people all around the world whose lives have somehow been affected by organ donation and transplant medicine. I don't always feel that as an actor my job is that important or relevant. But, I soon realized that *Three Rivers* would be a source of great comfort to those aforementioned people providing perhaps for the first time an accurate and cathartic experience directly related to that which they all shared."[42] Barbee shared in a 2010 interview that, "Alex was fantastic. In the beginning, though, he was worried about playing a doctor. He was concerned that he couldn't pull it off. I said, 'I want you to talk to Gonzo, then let's talk about this again.'"[43] As O'Loughlin had confirmed in a prior interview with connectv.com, "Whenever I play a role, I try to immerse myself in it. But this seemed so immense to get to any sort of level of honesty and truth. I didn't think I could pull it off."[44] Barbee revealed, "Then, Alex became so tight with Gonzo. He went to Cleveland to hang out with him, and they became buddies. Once he met Gonzo, and he could picture his patterns and behavior after a real person, he was fine. Alex was just a total treasure. I loved his commitment. Then he became part of Donate Life. He became so moved by the whole thing that he wanted to go further. He wanted to be a spokesperson for them."[45] Tenaya Wallace, then Expert Consultant for the Donate Life - Hollywood chapter, shared, "Alex said to me that he was very attracted to the part of this physician as a transplant surgeon, because he felt like he could do something to help people through this role. He asked Carol Barbee if he could talk to somebody about promoting organ donation. So, I went to the set, and he told me he wanted to do more than just be a spokesperson. He wanted to become an Ambassador for Donate Life. I told him if he were in the role of an Ambassador, he would have to be trained. He did not hesitate one bit. He said, 'Let's set it up.' So, we did. Part of the training involved learning about the donating process, its myths and misconceptions, and part of it involved how to speak with people eloquently about organ donation. One of Alex's suggestions to me was that we need to do more on a national level. That was one of the reasons we set up our

Alex O'Loughlin takes time to speak with the press (photo credit: Meryl Hollar, from the author's personal collection)

national campaign to register '20 Million in 2012.' The entertainment industry is a very valuable resource for spreading the word and getting people to take action. The truth is, while *Three Rivers* was on the air, nationwide registration for organ donation rose 6%."[46] But O'Loughlin wasn't done. On June 11, 2010, at the Paley Center in Beverly Hills, as part of the Donate Life Film Festival, Donate Life Hollywood formally presented him with the Donate Life Person of the Year Award, which serves as a 'thank you' to those who have helped so much.[47] While at the event, O'Loughlin was inspired by Todd Storch, whose 13 year-old daughter had been killed in a skiing accident and subsequently saved the lives of five people through organ donation. Storch had set up the Taylor's Gift Foundation in her memory and honor to help spread the word about organ donation. O'Loughlin was so touched by this that he volunteered to be a spokesman for Taylor's Gift. Storch shared that, "Tara, my wife, and I got a chance to meet with Alex. He really connected with the work we're trying

Alex O'Loughlin shares press time with the author
(from the author's personal collection)

to do, and we became friends. He has been fantastic in helping our cause and what we're trying to accomplish in trying to make a really big impact across the US, trying to turn a negative into a positive."[48]

Even while O'Loughlin was in California to receive the Donate Life award, he had already been signed to play McGarrett on the reboot of *Hawaii Five-O*. In an interview with "The Star-Advertiser's" Mike Gordon, Peter Lenkov talked about the first time he met O'Loughlin, "Alex had just gotten off a plane. He had two days' scruff on him and had on a leather jacket. We were sitting next to each other on a couch and I remember looking at him and thinking, 'He's an action hero.' When I wrote *Five-0,* and we started casting, we met and talked about it, and I thought, 'He's the guy.' I knew right away."[49] And the importance of the role to the people of Hawaii wasn't lost on O'Loughlin, as he shared with "In Style" magazine, "It's important that we honestly represent this culture and the Hawaiian people, who have welcomed us. As an Aussie playing this hugely iconic American character, I feel truly honored. Thanks for trusting me."[50] Needless to say, O'Loughlin took the role, and the series is now at the time of writing, in its sixth season.

Co-star Taryn Manning spoke about what it's like working with O'Loughlin, "There's such great chemistry. I love Alex. I think he's so kind, and I think he works so hard, incredibly hard. I know he does the bulk of his own stunts. Larry Teng (Director) showed me the dailies of 'Ohuna' (The Secret)[51] and a stunt Alex did, and I was like, 'Is that Alex?' That's what I love about him. He *is* this guy. On top of it all, you can't trace his accent at all. But, the minute we 'cut,' he gets right back into his Australian accent. You're just like, 'Wow, you're amazing.' I truly, truly love that. He's a good guy. And, any day he might seem a little 'off,' he's a human being. He's tired. He works very, very hard, and I have a lot of respect for that. Alex and I have cultivated a rapport. He trusts me, and I trust him. I think that we both trust that natural chemistry that we have that you just can't explain when two actors or people come together. It just works. I see him, and we high five, and we hug. And he's like, 'what's up?' He's very funny. He'll start singing one of my songs and make me laugh. He always wants to hear my music. It's also really nice to see him smile on screen, because he's under so much stress in the character. Yeah, I like the smiles brought out by Mary."[52]

The man himself told "In Style" magazine in 2011, "McGarrett is the hardest character I've ever played because he is so serious."[53] O'Loughlin is also a certified stuntman in Australia with martial arts skills,[54] trained in Kung Fu, Tai Chi,[55] and jiu-jitsu. He started studying Shobukai karate in Australia at the age of six and earned a brown belt by the age of 10, saying, "It was a huge part of my life, man. I wouldn't miss it." He also enjoys running, and circuit training.[56] While

Top: Alex O'Loughlin in a candid moment (photo credit: Meryl Hollar, from the author's personal collection)
Bottom: Alex O'Loughlin speaks candidly with the author (from the author's personal collection

working on *Moonlight,* he told thetvaddict.com that he probably did 75% of his own stunts.[57]

While the demands of such a series have obviously made it difficult for O'Loughlin to resume his spokesperson duties for the aforementioned Donate Life, the author was delighted to find that his passion for the project has not waned. When asked during some one-on-one time with the author[58] why he thought having a platform was important for an actor, O'Loughlin shared, "I'd like to preface that by saying I wish I had more time. This is the most demanding show I've ever been on. It's been the most incredible roller coaster ride. I've had personal conflict; I've had personal injury. And, I was never prepared for a show like this and for the demands of a show like this. So, I look forward to the time when I have more time to get back into my service work that's so important to me and to my family. Personally, for this actor, there are so many reasons why it's important to have a platform. I don't know where to start. It's like, 'What's the meaning of life? service, right?' Without service, you have nothing. It's a terribly hard thing to answer, because today there's so much self-help and other books on the shelf, and all those books are probably about what people are searching for – the truth. And what I do for a living, all this can be construed as like something that's based on vanity. It's not important. I mean, I do appreciate it, and I love it, but you've gotta do for others. I'm involved in a big network show at the moment. It is what it is, and it fits where it fits. I think after this what I'd really like to do is go to sort of smaller stories that speak to me on a personal level and challenge people in other ways that maybe this show doesn't. Do you know what I mean? I'd like to sort of take a step away."

Going forward, whatever opportunities await this talented and unpredictable Aussie in his return to the service work for which he is so passionate and to the production of stories and challenges of his own remain to be seen.

W • DID YOU KNOW • DID YOU KNOW • DID YOU KNOW • DID YOU KNOW • DID YOU K

O'Loughlin worked as an extra and appeared in a few commercials (i. e. , Mitsubishi, Toyota, and Tampons Libra) before heading to NIDA.[59]

O'Loughlin has been a registered organ donor since he was a teenager.[60]

O'Loughlin has studied accents since he was a child,[62] *and in* Man-Thing, *he masters (in the author's opinion) the very difficult Southern accent.*

O'Loughlin is known for his modesty, and, in an October 17, 2009 MySpace entry, he wrote, "I humbly appreciate all the support I constantly receive."

O'Loughlin was photographed for Darren Tieste's work The Beauty Book *for Brain Cancer.*

O'Loughlin was involved at the beginning of 2013 with a charity event to save the Coastlines of Hawaii (http://sustainablecoastlines. org) and in April, 2013 with a Relay for Life event at the University of Hawaii, Manoa to raise breast cancer awareness.

O'Loughlin has co-taught two women's self-defense classes to date with former Mixed Martial Arts Champion Egan Inoue to raise money for the Kapiolani Medical Center for Women and Children.

ENDNOTES

Notes to chapter 1

1. "Memories of Hawaii Five-O." Emme's Isand Moments. CBS. KGMB-TV, Honolulu 20 October 1996.
2. Virginia Tolles, "Memories of 'Hawaii Five-O,'" http://www.memoriesofhawaiifive-O.com (accessed May 21, 2014).
3. Coopersmith, Jerome. "Book 'em Danno! My Years Writing for Hawaii Five-O." Mystery Scene Spring 2004.
4. Coopersmith, Jerome. "Book 'em Danno! My Years Writing for Hawaii Five-O." Mystery Scene Spring 2004.
5. Raddatz, Leslie. "How An Ex-Rodeo Rider Went West to Enjoy the Good Life as a Hawaiian Cop." TV Guide January 4, 1969.
6. Dowsett, Terry. "Re: Did You Get This Email Re: Hawaii Five-0?" Message to Cheryl Hollar. 23 January 2013. Email.
7. The first was Barbara Eden in an I Dream of Jeannie episode.
8. "Classic TV & Movie Hits," http://classic-tv.com/ratings/1967-1968-tv-show-ratings.html (accessed May 21, 2014). And "Classic TV Database," http://www.classictvhits.com (accessed May 21, 2014).
9. "Memories of Hawaii Five-O." Emme's Isand Moments. CBS. KGMB-TV, Honolulu 20 October 1996.
10. IMDb. Web. http://www.imdb.com/title/tt0062568 (accessed May 21, 2014).
11. Memories of Hawaii Five-O." Emme's Isand Moments. CBS. KGMB-TV, Honolulu 20 October 1996.
12. Doug Nye, "James MacArthur's Work Goes Far Beyond 'Book 'em Danno,'" Chicago Tribune 15 March 2007: Lifestyles.
13. Coopersmith, Jerome. "Book 'em Danno! My Years Writing for Hawaii Five-O." Mystery Scene Spring 2004.
14. Virginia Tolles, "Memories of 'Hawaii Five-O,'" http://www.memoriesofhawaiifive-O.com (accessed May 21, 2014).
15. The Hollywood Reporter. August 12, 2008. http://www.hollywoodreporter.com/news/cbs-plans-20-version-five-117313.
16. The Hollywood Reporter. October 8, 2009. http://www.mjq.net/fiveo/hollywoodreporter-8oct09.htm.
17. The Star Advertiser. November 19, 2010. <http://www.staradvertiser.com/columnists/20101119_Peter_Lenkov.html?id=109126329.>
18. The Star Advertiser. December 29, 2010. http://www.staradvertiser.com/news/20101229_TV_producer_pours_passion_into_Five-0.html?id=112593909.
19. Dawsett, Terry. "Re: Did You Get This Email re: Hawaii Five-0?" Message to Cheryl Hollar. 23 January 2013. Email.
20. "Ohana" (Family). Hawaii Five-0. CBS. KGMB-TV, Honolulu 27 September 2010.
21. "Malama Ka 'Aina" (Respect the Land). Hawaii Five-0. CBS. KGMB-TV, Honolulu 4 October 2010.
22. Cheryl Hollar, http://www.mytakeontv.com/2015/01/30/saber-ops-military-advisors-to-hawaii-five-0-and-beyond/, "Saber Ops: Military Advisors to Hawaii Five-0 and Beyond," January 30, 2015.

Notes to chapter 2

1. State of Hawaii Film Office. Web. http://filmoffice.hawaii.gov/hawaii-celebrates-century-of-film-production-in-the-islands/ (accessed June 5, 2014).
2. The Star Bulletin. September 10, 1999. <http://archives.starbulletin.com/1999/09/10/news/story5.html>
3. Spangler, Stephanie G. Telephone interview. 1 April 2013.
4. Spangler, Randy. Telephone interview. 19 March 2013.
5. "honoluluadvertiser.com," http://the.honoluluadvertiser.com/article/2004/Dec/12/il/il01a.html (accessed June 5, 2014).
6. Spangler, Stephanie G. Telephone interview. 1 April 2013.
7. Ibid.
8. Ibid.
9. The series never made it to production.
10. Spangler, Stephanie. Telephone interview. 1 April 2013.
11. Ibid.
12. Ibid.
13. Ibid.
14. Triplett, Jim. Telephone interview. 28 February 2013.
15. Ibid.
16. Chinn, Timmy. Telephone interview. 28 May 2015.
17. Spangler, Stephanie. Telephone interview. 1 April 2013.
18. Ibid.

19. Ibid.
20. Ibid.
21. Ibid.
22. Ibid.
23. Triplett, Jim. Telephone interview. 28 February 2013.
24. Ibid.
25. Ibid.
26. Chinn, Timmy. Telephone interview. 28 May 2015.
27. Ibid.
28. Ibid.
29. Ibid.
30. Ibid.
31. Ibid.
32. Ibid.

Notes to chapter 3

1. Spangler, Randy. Telephone interview. 19 March 2013.
2. Kia, Kahu Blaine Kamalani. Telephone interview. 4 March 2013.
3. Bishaw, Kahu Kelekona. Telephone interview. 1 March 2013.
4. Kekuna, Kahu Curtis Pa'alua Kwai Fong. Telephone interview. 4 August 2011.
5. Bishaw, Kahu Kelekona. Telephone interview. 1 March 2013.
6. "Hawaii Five-0 Season Two Blessing." Hawaii News Now Live Stream. Hawaii News Now, 11 July 2011. Web. 11 July 2011.
7. Kekuna, Kahu Curtis Pa'alua Kwai Fong. Telephone interview. 4 August 2011.
8. Kia, Kahu Blaine Kamalani. Telephone interview. March 4, 2013.
9. Cheryl Hollar, http://www.mytakeontv.com/2013/07/16/hawaii-five-0-comes-home-to-shoot-season-four, "Hawaii Five-0 Comes Home to Shoot Season Four," July 16, 2013.
10. Cheryl Hollar. http://www.mytakeontv.com/2014/07/11/hawaii-five-0-holds-season-five-blessing, "Hawaii Five-0 Holds Season Five Blessing," July 11, 2014.
11. Season Two, Episode 12.
12. Cheryl Hollar, http://www.mytakeontv.com/2015/07/15/hawaii-blesses-first-day-of-filming-season-six-of-hawaii-five-0/, "Hawaii Blesses First Day of Filming Season Six of Hawaii Five-0," July 15, 2015.
13. Harrington, Al. Telephone interview. June 5, 2013.
14. Cheryl Hollar, http://www.mytakeontv.com/2013/07/16/hawaii-five-0-comes-home-to-shoot-season-four, "Hawaii Five-0 Comes Home to Shoot Season Four," July 16, 2013.
15. Cheryl Hollar, http://www.mytakeontv.com/2014/07/11/hawaii-five-0-holds-season-five-blessing, "Hawaii Five-0 Holds Season Five Blessing, July 11, 2014.

Notes to chapter 4

1. Maduli, Janet Lee. "Re: Sunset on the Beach." Message to Cheryl Hollar. 13 June 2013. Email.
2. Ibid.
3. "hawaiimagazine.com," http://www.hawaiimagazine.com/blogs/hawaii_today/2010/9/14/scenes_from_Hawaii_Five_0_Premiere_Waikiki (accessed May 21, 2014).
4. James MacArthur Official Website. Web. http://www.jamesmacarthur.com/SunsetontheBeach/Remarks.shtml (accessed May 21, 2014).
5. "staradvertiser.com," http://tgif.staradvertiser.com/archives/8026 (accessed May 21, 2014).
6. "hawaiimagazine.com," http://www.hawaiimagazine.com/blogs/hawaii_today/2010/9/14/scenes_from_Hawaii_Five_0_premiere_Waikiki/3 (accessed May 21, 2014).
7. "nonstophonolulu.com," http://www.nonstophonolulu.com/stories/live-hawaii-five-o-premiere-sunset-on-the-beach/ (accessed May 21, 2014). "staradvertiser.com," http://www.staradvertiser.com/features/20110630_Five-0_on_the_beach.html?id=124762259 (accessed May 21, 2014).
8. "nonstophonolulu.com," http://www.nonstophonolulu.com/blogs/hawaii-five-0-premiere-sunset-on-the-beach (accessed May 21, 2014).
9. "Ina Paha," If Perhaps aired on November 7, 2014.
10. Doversola, Margaret. Telephone interview. 14 April 2013. Harrington, Al. Telephone interview. 5 June 2013.
11. Margaret Doversola. Telephone interview. April 14, 2013.
12. Hawaii Five-0. Web. http://www.hawaiifive0.org/premier.shtml (accessed August 5, 2014).
13. James MacArthur Official website. Web. http://www.jamesmacarthur.com/SiteIntro.shtml (accessed May 21, 2014).

14. "hawaiimagazine.com." http://www.hawaiimagazine.com/blogs/hawaii_today/2010/1/14/ABC_Lost_final_season_debut_Waikiki (accessed May 21, 2014).

Notes to chapter 5

1. "imdb.com," http://www.imdb.com/title/tt0062568/fullcredits?ref_=tt_ov_st_sm (accessed April 1, 2013).
2. Ibid.
3. "imdb.com," http://www.imdb.com/title/tt1600194/?ref_=fn_al_tt_1 (accessed April 1, 2013).
4. Steve Boyum information from: Boyum, Steve. Telephone interview. 27 November 2012.
5. Joe Dante information from: Dante, Joe. Telephone interviews. 16 November 2012, 23 April 2013.
6. Episode Three, "Kanalu Hope Loa" (The Last Break); Episode Six, "Ho'oma'ike" (Unmasked); and Episode Sixteen, "Nanahu" (Embers).
7. At press time, Episode Three, "Ua 'o'oloku ke anu i na mauna" (The Chilling Storm is on the Mountains) and Episode Six, "Na Pilikua Nui" (Monsters).

Notes to chapter 6

1. Doversola, Margaret. Telephone interview.
2. IMDb.com. Web. http://www.imdb.com/title/tt0062568/?ref_=nv_sr_2 (accessed August 6, 2014).
3. IMDb.com. Web. http://www.imdb.com/title/tt1600194/?ref_=nv_sr_1 (accessed August 6, 2014).
4. Virginia Tolles, "Memories of 'Hawaii Five-O'," http://www.memoriesofhawaiifive-0.com/belovedsemiregulars.htm (accessed May 21, 2014).
5. Aiu, Rod. Telephone interview. 8 April 2013.
6. Ibid.
7. Doversola, Margaret. Telephone interview. 14 April 2013. Harrington, Al. Telephone interview. 5 June 2013.
8. IMDb.com. Web. http://www.imdb.com/title/tt0062568/?ref_=nv_sr_2 (accessed August 6, 2014). IMDb.com. Web. http://www.imdb.com/title/tt1600194/?ref_=nv_sr_1 (accessed August 6, 2014).
9. Taryn Manning information from: Manning, Taryn. Telephone interview. 21 November 2012.
10. "Ohuna" (The Secret). Hawaii-Five-0. CBS. KGMB-TV, Honolulu 19 November 2012.
11. Season Five, Episode 7, "Ina Paha" (If Perhaps)
12. Mark Dacascos information from: Dacascos, Mark. Telephone interview. 3 June 2013.
13. "easyukulele.com," http://www.easyukulele.com/moe-keale.html (accessed June 5, 2014).
14. IMDb.com. Web. http://www.imdb.com/title/tt0062568/?ref_=nv_sr_2 (accessed August 6, 2014).
15. IMDb.com. Web. http://www.imdb.com/title/tt0062568/?ref_=nv_sr_2 (accessed August 6, 2014). IMDb.com. Web. http://www.imdb.com/title/tt1600194/?ref_=nv_sr_1 (accessed August 6, 2014).
16. Keale, Carol Miller. "Moe Keale." Message to Cheryl Hollar. 15 August 2013. Email.
17. The Hollywood Reporter. November 21, 2013. <http://www.hollywoodreporter.com/live-feed/hawaii-five-0s-chi-mcbride-658456>
18. The Los Angeles Times. March 19, 2012. http://articles.latimes.com/2012/mar/19/entertainment/la-et-ed-asner-20120319. "Kaleie" (Faith). Hawaii Five-0. CBS. KGMB-TV, Honolulu 19 March 2012.Kanalua" (Doubt). Hawaii Five-0. CBS. KGMB-TV, Honolulu 1 October 2012. "Wooden Model of a Rat." Hawaii Five-O. CBS. KGMB-TV, Honolulu 11 December 1975.
19. Episodes include "Ma Ke Kahakai" (Shore), Season One, Episode 20; Ua aihue" (Stolen), Season Five, Episode 11; and "Hoa 'inea" (Misery Loves Company), Season Six, Episode 14.

Notes to chapter 7

1. IMDb. Web. http://www.imdb.com/name/nm0958602/?ref_=nv_sr_6 (accessed December 3, 2014).
2. Hawaii Five-O Convention.
3. James MacArthur was honored at this Film Festival. More about this will be revealed in Chapter Nine - A.
4. Native Hawaiian.
5. Pickard, Jerry. "The Zulu Questions." Message to Cheryl Hollar. 4 July 2013. Email.
6. Pickard, Jerry. "The Zulu Questions." Message to Cheryl Hollar. 4 July 2013. Email.
7. Referencing righteousness.
8. Pickard, Jerry. "The Zulu Questions." Message to Cheryl Hollar. 4 July 2013. Email.
9. IMDb. Web. http://www.imdb.com/name/nm0364228/?ref_=nv_sr_1 (accessed December 3, 2014).
10. Harrington, Al. Telephone interview. 5 June 2013.
11. IMDb. Web. http://www.imdb.com/name/nm0958602/?ref_=nv_sr_6 (accessed December 3, 2014). All Zulu information from: Pickard, Jerry. "The Zulu Questions." Message to Cheryl Hollar. 4 July 2013. Email.
12. All Zulu information from: Pickard, Jerry. "The Zulu Questions." Message to Cheryl Hollar. 4 July 2013. Email.
13. Al Harrington information from: Harrington, Al. Telephone interview. 5 June 2013.

14. For this chapter: Cheryl Hollar, http://www.mytakeontv.com/2012/12/19/hawaii-five-0s-kono-grace-park-gets-real-with-my-take-on-tv/, "Hawaii Five-0's Kono, Grace Park, Gets Real with My Take on TV," December 19, 2012.

Notes to chapter 8

1. "Alone Together." Three Rivers. CBS. KGMB-TV, Honolulu. 1 November 2009.
2. Fong's first acting was in a feature film called Ghost of the China Sea in 1958: IMDb. Web. http://www.imdb.com/name/nm0284578/?ref_=fn_al_nm (accessed December 4, 2014).
3. "Brief Lives: A Tribute to Kam Fong Chun." James MacArthur, Remembering Kam Fong Chun. BBC. Radio 5, Honolulu. 10 November 2002.
4. Ibid.
5. Ibid.
6. IMDb. Web. http://www.imdb.com/name/nm0284578/?ref_=fn_al_nm_1 (accessed December 4, 2014).
7. Wendie Burbridge, "Five-O Redux: Honoring Kam Fong," Hawaii Five-0 Blog, May 29, 2013.
8. IMDb. Web. http://www.imdb.com/name/nm0284578/?ref_=fn_al_nm_1 (accessed December 4, 2014).
9. Ibid.
10. Ibid.
11. Mike Gordon and Rod Ohira, "'Five-O' Actor Kam Fong Chun Dead at 84," October 30, 2002.
12. Ibid.
13. "A Death in the Family." Hawaii Five-O. CBS. KGMB-TV, Honolulu 4 May 1978.
14. Mike Gordon and Rod Ohira, "'Five-O Actor Kam Fong Chun Dead at 84," October 30, 2002.
15. Wendie Burbridge, "Five-0 Redux: Honoring Kam Fong," Hawaii Five-0 Blog, May 29, 2013.
16. Ibid.
17. IMDb. Web. http://www.imdb.com/name/nm0284578/?ref_=fn_al_nm_1 (accessed December 4, 2014).
18. Ibid.
19. "Brief Lives: A Tribute to Kam Fong Chun." James MacArthur, Remembering Kam Fong Chun. BBC. Radio 5, Honolulu. 10 November 2002.
20. IMDb. Web. http://www.imdb.com/name/nm0196654/bio (accessed December 16, 2014).
21. Web. http://www.starpulse.com/Actors/Kim,_Daniel_Dae/Biography/ (accessed December 16, 2014).
22. Web. http://unitedagents.co.uk/daniel-dae-kim (accessed December 16, 2014).
23. Web, http://www.starpulse.com/Actors/Kim,_Daniel_Dae/Biography/ (accessed December 16, 2014).
24. Web, http://unitedagents.co.uk/daniel-dae-kim (accessed December 16, 2014).
25. Web, http://www.mahalo.com/daniel-dae-kim/ (accessed December 16, 2014).
26. Web, http://www.famright.com/quotes/Daniel-Dae-Kim.html (accessed December 16, 2014).
27. Christie, Wilson, http://www.honolulupulse.com/2011/02/daniel-dae-kim-headlines-hty-fundraiser/, "Daniel Dae Kim Headlines HTY Fundraiser," February 11, 2011.
28. Web, http://movies.msn.com/celebrities/celebrity-biography/daniel-dae-kim/ (accessed December 16, 2014).
29. Web, http://www.royalalberthall.com/tickets/the-king-and-i/default.aspx (accessed December 16, 2014).
30. Cheryl Hollar, http://www.mytakeontv.com/2013/10/08/hawaii-five-0-sunset-brings-dawn-of-season-four/, "Hawaii Five-0: Sunset Brings Dawn of Season Four," October 8, 2013.
31. Web, http://www.starpulse.com/Actors/Kim,_Daniel_Dae/Biography/ (accessed December 16, 2014).
32. http://www.hancinema.net/-lost-star-daniel-dae-kim-meets-fans-in-yeosu-44823.html, "Lost Star Daniel Dae Kim Meets Fans in Yeosu," July 5, 2012.
33. Christie Wilson, http://www.honolulupulse.com/2011/02/daniel-dae-kim-headlines-hty-fundraiser/, 'Daniel Dae Kim Headlines HTY Fundraiser," February 11, 2011.
34. Ken Beck, http://americanprofile.com/articles/daniel-dae-kim-hawaii-five-o/, "Daniel Dae Kim of Hawaii Five-0."
35. Web, Daniel Dae Kim's official website, http://danieldaekim.com/about (accessed December 16, 2014).
36. Denise Petski, http://deadline.com/2015/08/daniel-dae-kim-mike-kims-escaping-north-korea-feature-film-1201507291/, "Daniel Dae Kim Develping 'Escaping North Korea' Memoir as Feature Film," August 26, 2015.
37. Web, http://www.starpulse.com/Actors/Kim,_Daniel_Dae/Biography/ (accessed December 16, 2014).
38. Christie Wilson, http://www.honolulupulse.com/2011/02/daniel-dae-kim-headlines-hty-fundraiser/, "Daniel Dae Kim Headlines HTY Fundraiser," February 11, 2011.
39. Web, http://www.tv.com/people/daniel-dae-kim/trivia/ (accessed December 16, 2014).
40. http://www.hancinema.net/-lost-star-daniel-dae-kim-meets-fans-in-yeosu-44823.html, "Lost Star Daniel Dae Kim Meets Fans in Yeosu," July 5, 2012.
41. Pacific Business News, http://www.bizjournals.com/pacific/news/2010/12/17/daniel-dae-kim-sells-interest-in-the.html, "Daniel Dae Kim Sells Stake in The Counter, December 17, 2010.
42.

43. The Deadline Team, http://deadline.com/2014/07/daniel-dae-kims-3ad-development-executives-lindsay-goffman-keo-lee-800326/, "Daniel Dae Kim's 3AD Adds Development Duo," July 7, 2014.

Notes to chapter 9
1. Harrington, Al. Telephone interview. 5 June 2013.
2. Doversola, Margaret. Telephone interview. 14 April 2013.
3. Web, http://jamesmacarthur.com (accessed December 16, 2014).
4. Web, http://jamesmacarthur.com (accessed December 16, 2014).
5. Rhodes, Karen. "Re: Hawaii Five-O." Message to Cheryl Hollar. 30 April 2013. Email.
6. MacArthur passed away on October 28, 2010
7. IMDb. Web. http://www.imdb.com/name/nm0004790/?ref_=nv_sr_1 (accessed January 12, 2015).
8. Patricia Foster Rye, LA Stage Times, "Scott Caan Finds His Way Around," June 1, 2012.
9. The Los Angeles Times, "The Sunday Conversation: Melanie Griffith Returns to the Stage," July 1, 2012.
10. Lauren also directed the play and appeared in the Season One Finale of the series reboot, "Oia'l'o" (Trust).
11. Appeared in Season One, Episode 23 of the reboot series, "Ua Hiki PMai Kapalena Pau" (Until the End Is Near)
12. Val Lauren and Bre Blair also star in this project.
13. Patricia Foster Rye, "LA Stage Times," Scott Caan Finds His Way Around, June 1, 2012.
14. James Caan appeared in the reboot Five-0 in Season Two, Episode 18, "Lekio" (Radio).
15. Web. http://www.filmbug.com/db/3417 (accessed January 12, 2015).
16. According to filmbug.com, this was the winner of the Critics Award at the 2003 CineVegas International Film Festival
17. IMDb. Web. http://www.imdb.com/name/nm0004790/?ref_=fn_al_nm_1 (accessed January 12, 2015).
18. Ibid.
19. Web. http://surfershealing.org (accessed January 12, 2015).
20. Web. http://liferollson.org (accessed Jauary 12, 2015).
21. Adam Preskill, "Life Rolls On Helps Surfers with Disabilities," Los Angeles Confidential, N.D.
22. This footnote and previous "Did You Know…" from Patricia Foster Rye, "LA Stage Times," Scott Caan Finds His Way Around, June 1, 2012.
23. IMDb. Web. http://www.imdb.com/name/nm0788218/?ref_=fn_al_nm_1 accessed January 12, 2015.
24. Markus A. Larr, http://www.starpulse.com/news/Markus_A_Larr/2013/08/17/melanie_griffith_signs_to_play_scott_c, "Melanie Griffith Signs to Play Scott Caan's Mom On Hawaii Five-0, August 17, 2013.

Notes to chapter 10
1. Doversola, Margaret. Telephone interview. 14 April 2013.
2. Relating to Hawaii and its customs and people
3. As opposed to "New York" or "back East" crimes, "Hawaiian" crimes were typical of the region of Hawaii.
4. Jack Lord, "Aloha 'Oe" (Love You), ASTA Holiday, "Jack Lord, Holiday's Lord of the Leis in Hawaii," May, 1977.
5. John Fischer, http://gohawaii.about.com/cs/hawaii_radio/a/jack_lord.htm, "Jack Lord A Look at the Man and His Relationship with Hawaii."
6. Jack Lord, "Aloha 'Oe" (Love You), ASTA Holiday, "Jack Lord, Holiday's Lord of the Leis in Hawaii," May, 1977.
7. From a blog by President and CEO of PBS Hawaii Leslie Wilcox, September 9, 2008.
8. Appeared in original series in over 25 episodes from 1968-1979; appeared in reboot series in Season Two, Episode Ten, "Ki'ilua" (Deceiver).
9. Actor Stephen Boyd was one of these.
10. Kinau Wilder was the mother of Don Ho's manager, Kimo Wilder McVay.
11. Unique to Hawaii, Borges music was jazz, similar to Frank Sinatra and Tony Bennett.
12. Jimmy Borges information from: Borges, Jimmy. Telephone interview. 2 July 2013.
13. Season Eight, Episode 18, "Loose Ends Get Hit"
14. Keale, Carol Miller. "Moe Keale." Message to Cheryl Hollar. 15 August 2013. Email
15. Web, http://www.jack-lord.info (accessed February 2, 2015).
16. Web, http://www.imdb.com/name/nm0520437/?ref_=fn_al_nm_1 (accessed February 2, 2015).
17. Aiu, Rod. Telephone interview. 8 April 2013.
18. Spangler, Randy. Telephone interview. 19 March 2013.
19. Doversola, Margaret. Telephone interview. 14 April 2013.
20. "Did You Know" information, unless otherwise cited, from IMDb.com. Web. https://pro-labs.imdb.com/name/nm0520437/trivia?ref_=nm_subnv_persdet_trivia (accessed November 6, 2015).
21. Jack Lord, "Aloha 'Oe," (Love You), ASTA Holiday, "Jack Lord, Holiday's Lord of the Leis in Hawaii, May 1977.
22. Keale, Carol Miller. "Moe Keale." Message to Cheryl Hollar. 26 January 2016. Email.
23. Keale, Carol Miller. "Moe Keale." Message to Cheryl Hollar. 15 August 2013. Email.

24. As credited in earlier work in Australia White Collar Blue, The Oyster Farmer, Love Bytes, Blackjack: Sweet Science, and Man-Thing (IMDb. Web. http://www.imdb.com/name/nm1533927/?ref_=sr_1 (accessed January 8, 2015).

25. IMDb. Web. http://www.imdb.com/name/nm1533927/?ref_=sr_1 (accessed January 8, 2015).

26. Fransesca Scorcucchi, "Vanity Fair Italia," 26 May 2010.

27. "The Canberra Times," 28 June 2005.

28. Fransesca Scorcucchi, "Vanity Fair Italia," 26 May 2010.

29. "The Courier Mail," 23 June 2005, "The Canberra Times," 28 June 2005; IMDb. Web. http://www.imdb.com/name/nm1533927/?ref_=sr_1 (accessed January 8, 2015).

30. "The Canberra Times," 28 June 2005.

31. Amy Kaufman, "Los Angeles Times," April 27, 2010.

32. "The Australian," November 2, 2005.

33. Ibid.

34. http://connectv.com, October 14, 2009.

35. IMDb. Web. http://www.imdb.com/name/nm1533927/?ref_=sr_1 (accessed January 8, 2015).

36. Amrie Cunningham, http://mytakeontv.wordpress.com/2009/04/29/alex-oloughlin-criminal-minds/, "Unsub with a Heart of Gold? Alex O'Loughlin Talks Criminal Minds," April 29, 2009.

37. Ibid.

38. Cheryl Hollar, http://suite101.com/article/three-rivers-and-family-guy-lead-impact-on-organ-donation-a397380, "TV Becomes Powerful Tool for Charities, Causes That Change Lives," November 23, 2011. (Reprinted at http://www.mytakeontv.com/author/cherylhollar).

39. September 6, 2009 entry

40. http://connectv.com, October 14, 2009.

41. December 1, 2009 entry

42. Cheryl Hollar, http://suite101.com/article/the-cbs-series-that-changed-a-generation-a403063, "The CBS Series That Changed a Generation," February 15, 2012. (Reprinted at http://www.mytakeontv.com/author/cherylhollar).

43. http://connectv.com, October 14, 2009.

44. Cheryl Hollar, http://suite101.com/article/the-cbs-series-that-changed-a-generation-a403063, "The CBS Series That Changed a Generation," February 15, 2012. (Reprinted at http://www.mytakeontv.com/author/cherylhollar).

45. Ibid.

46. Carol Barbee also was presented with the Crystal Heart Award at this event.

47. Cheryl Hollar, http://suite101.com/article/three-rivers-and-family-guy-lead-impact-on-organ-donation-a397380, "TV Becomes Powerful Tool for Charities, Causes That Change Lives, November 23, 2011. (Reprinted at http://www.mytakeontv.com/author/cherylhollar).

48. Mike Gordon, *The Star-Advertiser*, "Q&A with Peter Lenkov," February 3, 2012.

49. "InStyle," April, 2011.

50. Season Three, Episode 7, "Ohuna" (Secret).

51. Manning, Taryn. Telephone interview. 21 November 2012.

52. "InStyle," April, 2011.

53. Web. http://www.jamesmarsters.live.com/?page_id=227 (accessed January 8, 2015).

54. IMDb. Web. http://www.imdb.com/name/nm1533927/?ref_=sr_1 (accessed January 8, 2015).

55. Mark Morrison, "Men's Fitness," August, 2011.

56. Ibid.

57. Amrie Cunningham, http://www.thetvaddict.com/2007/11/23/thetvaddictcom-interview-moonlight-star-alex-oloughlin/, "The tvaddict.com Interview: Moonlight Star Alex O'Loughlin," November 23, 2007.

58. Cheryl Hollar, http://www.mytakeontv.com/2013/10/11/alex-oloughlin-hawaii-five-0s-actor-with-a-vision/, "Alex O'Loughlin: *Hawaii Five-0*'s Actor with a Vision," October 11, 2013.

59. "The Canberra Times," June 28, 2005.

60. http://connectv.com, October 14, 2009.

61. Amrie Cunningham, http://www.thetvaddict.com/2007/11/23/thetvaddictcom-interview-moonlight-star-alex-oloughlin, "TheTVaddict.com Interview: *Moonlight* Star Alex O'Loughlin," November 23, 2007.

About the Author

Cheryl Hollar is a freelance writer for the entertainment industry and covers everything from the TCA's to red-carpet events to set visits to celebrity charities. Her work includes coverage of Mark Harmon's Annual Charity Baseball event helping the children of Oklahoma as well as a series of pieces on the impact television has on changing people's lives through organ donation. Cheryl has also been commissioned to write pieces for an LA group of family magazines, including specialneeds.com and familychoiceawards.com. Currently a contributing writer at mytakeontv.com, Cheryl holds a Certificate in Writing for Television from UCLA's Writers' Extension Program. She is no stranger to the industry, having worked in public relations in New York City for Rogers & Cowan and Bon Jovi Productions (McGhee Entertainment). Cheryl is a member of the Christian Women in Media Association and the Hollywood Prayer Network. She is also a member of the International Twins Association, where she has served as President and/or Vice-President with her twin sister at conventions across the United States. Cheryl loves animals, traveling, writing, and meeting new people.